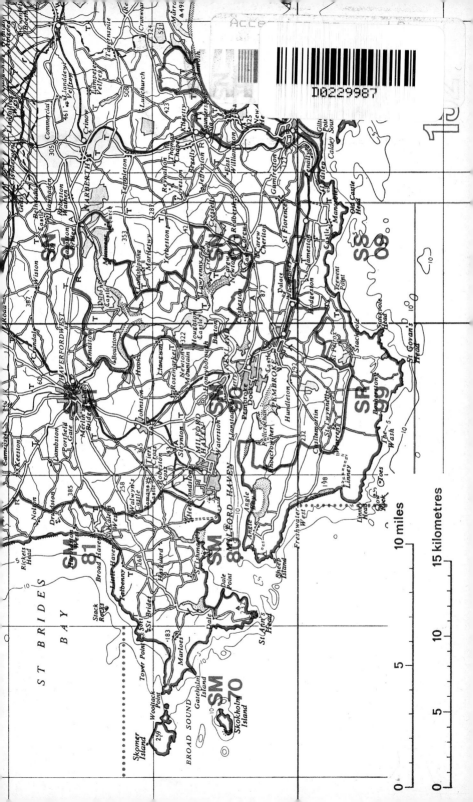

PEMBROKESHIRE COAST

NATIONAL PARK GUIDE NO. 10

EDITED BY
DILLWYN MILES

ISSUED FOR THE
COUNTRYSIDE COMMISSION

LONDON
HER MAJESTY'S STATIONERY OFFICE
1973

SBN 11 700348 4

ACKNOWLEDGEMENTS

The Editor wishes to acknowledge the co-operation received from the County Planning Officer of Pembrokeshire and his staff in the selection of photographs and in the preparation of maps; also from the staff of the Countryside Commission, who piloted the book through the press.

Acknowledgements are due to the following for the photographs reproduced in the book:

	PLATES
Crown copyright	1 2 5
Heather Angel	12 13
J. W. Donovan	10 11
Leonard and Marjorie Gayton	14 15 21 27
Dr J. K. St Joseph	3 18
Studio Jon	4 6 8 9 22 23 24 25 28 31 35 36 37 38
West Wales Naturalists' Trust	7
Roger Worsley	16 20 26 29 30 32 33 34

CONTENTS

v

ILLUSTRATIONS

PLATES

vii

FIGURES

The cover illustration is of Dinas in 1830, from a drawing by H. Gastineau engraved by E. Kennion.

PREFACE

IN APRIL, after too long an interval apart from necessarily brief excursions, I visited again the Pembrokeshire Coast National Park. I took with me recollections of a family holiday on Tenby's sands, of evening sun on cliffs at Huntsman's Leap and St. Bride's Haven, of a cliff walk to Saundersfoot in bluebell time; but none quite matched the fresh delight of walks along flower-garlanded cliffs of ancient rocks often spectacularly contorted, past harbours in narrow inlets and at the water's edge in sandy bays, all of which can now be reached by a footpath which runs, without interruption, for 167 miles.

Inland the county has been richly endowed by nature and by man, but its coasts are supreme. The islands and skerries are famous among ornithologists for the number and variety of the sea-birds. Seals can be seen, fishing and basking, along much of a coast notable for the richness of all kinds of marine life. Man has left his mark from the time when fact is so entangled with romantic legend that they are barely distinguishable. It is difficult to know whether archaeologist or historian will be most rewarded by visits to places, some of which were first inhabited at least twelve millennia ago. No intruders, not even the Romans, arrived in sufficient strength to obliterate traces of earlier cultures, although the Normans left a proud heritage of towns and castles. Wherever you go in the National Park, and whatever your country interests, with the aid of this guide-book you will find much to rivet your attention. Leave time also to enjoy beaches which have been attracting holiday visitors since the 1780s, and to sit on headlands where the air and fine scenery cannot fail to restore you.

The Pembrokeshire Coast is one of ten areas in England and Wales which have been designated as National Parks. These are specially administered, as described in Chapter 9 of this book, to ensure the preservation and enhancement of their natural beauty, while affording the best possible arrangements for your enjoyment of them. Please remember that many people live all the year round in this Pembrokeshire Coast National Park and depend on it for their livelihood. This is especially true of the farmers. The pleasure which you and they gain from your visit will depend in large measure on your observance of the Country Code which is included at the end of the book.

This guide has been written by men with exceptional knowledge of the county and their subjects. Dillwyn Miles is to be congratulated

ix

for having assembled such a distinguished team and for bringing together their work so skilfully. To him and them we are most grateful for a book which bears all the signs of, in the truest sense, a labour of love—love of a remarkable county which they help us all to share.

JOHN CRIPPS

July 1972

1

Introduction

by THE EDITOR

PEMBROKESHIRE is a peninsula, the most westerly in Wales. Tall cliffs and skerries protect it on three sides and landward lie stretches of mist-laden moorland. Here was the land of magic and enchantment, *Gwlad hud a lledrith*, where history and legend bemingle.

It was in the lovely vale of Cuch that Pwyll, Prince of Dyfed, drove off the hounds of another hunter and baited his own upon the captured stag, for which discourtesy he had to exchange places for a year with the indignant one, who was none other than the King of Annwn, the Celtic Other World. The paps of Presely preserve the memory of Arthur and his knights at Carn Arthur and Cerrig Marchogion, along with that of the bellicose sons of Owen of Pentre Ifan, who fought each other to a standstill with cudgels of oak on Carnedd Meibion Owen.

The Pembrokeshire Coast National Park was designated in 1952 and comprises the coastal belt, the upper reaches of Milford Haven, and the Presely Hills, covering 225 square miles (58,000 hectares) which is just over one-third of the area of the county.

In few places are gathered together such a diversity of scenery—majestic cliffs, concealed coves, smooth sands, wild moorland, rounded hills, tree-clad valleys, gambolling streams, island-studded seas. "Penbroch", said Giraldus Cambrensis, "is the finest part of the province of Demetia, and Demetia is the most beautiful in Wales".

Man has changed the face of Pembrokeshire so that little of the pristine landscape remains, save the cliff-faces and the smooth summits of the hills. For nearly 5,000 years he has shaped the environment. The field-walls he built at the dawn of the Christian era on St. David's Head and on Skomer are there today. The inscribed tombs of early Celtic saints and notables, used for centuries as rubbing stones and gateposts, have been removed to the shadow of churches founded by their contemporaries. Norman castles dot the county in various stages of decorous ruin, but five are still inhabited.

Much of the upland area is common land, grazed by sheep and wild mountain ponies. The Presely sheep are wintered on the military ranges at Castlemartin, where the breed of black cattle bearing that name originated. The smaller crofts have been swallowed by upland holdings which, in turn, are being absorbed by larger units. Dairy farming is pursued over most of the county, but in the south and west 8,000 acres are given to early potatoes. Turkey producing has taken an important place in the county's economy since the last war.

For close on two centuries, Pembrokeshire has been visited by those who wished to enjoy its beauty and its beaches. Since 1781 when John Jones, medical practitioner of Haverfordwest, promoted salutiferous sea-water baths at Tenby, that town has been a leading holiday resort; the rest of the county has followed its lead so that tourism is now one of its main industries, and people come from all parts to enjoy its peace and unspoilt beauty.

This is not a conventional guide-book: there is a selection of such books published by local authorities and by the Wales Tourist Board. It is, rather, a digest of the immensely varied geology, archaeology, history, and natural history of the Pembrokeshire Coast National Park; though, as these matters do not begin or end with the National Park, we have not been confined too rigidly by its boundaries. Our contributors are established authorities in their subjects, and they are all native to, or closely connected with, the county. Professor W. F. Grimes, Professor Neville George, Major Francis Jones, R. M. Lockley, T. A. Warren Davis, like the Editor, are of native stock; John Barrett and John Price have both given over twenty years of their expertise and devotion to the county; Robert Kennedy is the first curator of the long overdue county museum. It is an authoritative work for which those who want this kind of information are constantly clamouring. Its bibliography will help those who wish to gather further knowledge.

2

Geology and Scenery

by T. NEVILLE GEORGE

Geological history. Most of the rocks of Pembrokeshire are of ancient origin. They reveal a complex history, spanning several hundreds of million years, that included the deposition of sediments in great thickness, the accumulation of volcanic lavas and ashes, the repeated folding and faulting of the rocks by powerful earth-movements, and the moulding of a variety of landscapes by erosion. The youngest rocks, now forming a thin veneer of surface deposits, record the onset of arctic conditions during the Ice Age, and a final regional subsidence and a drowning of the coastal margins beneath the sea. The history is fragmented and its details are not easy to determine—they must be pieced together from residual evidence preserved in different parts of the Park, and not all of them are as yet fully known or fully understood.

In general distribution, the oldest rocks are exposed at the surface north of a line running from Druidston by Haverfordwest and Narberth to Whitland. They are mainly of Lower Palaeozoic age (about 570 to 400 million years old) and belong to the Cambrian, Ordovician, and Silurian systems; but in their midst older Pre-Cambrian rocks come to outcrop in a broken belt running eastwards from St. David's to Ambleston. Lower Palaeozoic rocks, locally with some Pre-Cambrian, also emerge from beneath younger rocks in the cores of sharp upfolds farther south, notably between Talbenny, Johnston, and Benton, between Skomer and St. Ishmael's, and between Freshwater West and St. Petrox. They have been greatly contorted and deformed by earth-movements.

In southern Pembrokeshire, on the other hand, the rocks are mainly of Upper Palaeozoic age (about 400 to 250 million years old) and belong to the Devonian and Carboniferous systems. They are represented by the Old Red Sandstone, the Carboniferous Limestone, the Millstone Grit, and the Coal Measures. They have been much folded and fractured, but not so acutely as the Lower Palaeozoic rocks. There also remain small pockets of Mesozoic and Tertiary rocks that were once extensive.

3

Unconsolidated glacial sands and gravels cover much of the ground. With the alluvium of the valleys they are a geologically late suite of deposits laid down only during the last few hundred thousand years. They scarcely mask the plateau form of a landscape that was sculptured in the Palaeozoic oldland and received its major definition in times long before the Glacial period.

Pre-Cambrian rocks. The oldest rocks of a proto-Pembrokeshire, the foundation on which all later rocks rest, are to be seen only in a few square miles of outcrop about St. David's, about Hayscastle, and about Benton. They prove to be volcanic ashes, with some lavas, whose visible thickness is of the order of 4,000 feet; and although the forms of the original volcanoes are no longer preserved—they were destroyed before the Cambrian rocks were deposited—the rocks (called Pebidian) imply an original landscape of active and explosive volcanic vents as the first recognisable stage of geological growth of the region.

The ashes and lavas originated in reservoirs of molten rock within the underlying crust. At a later time than the formation of the ashes, similar molten material in large volume was forced into the upper crustal layers without reaching the surface, and it there slowly cooled to form masses of granitic rocks. The bulging roof of the cover overlying the granites was removed by erosion in Pre-Cambrian times, and the granites (called Dimetian) now form small outcrops in the neighbourhood of St. David's itself, near Brawdy and Hayscastle, and for several miles east and west of Johnston.

Some of the ashes are fine-grained compact rocks, some frothy pumice, some coarse grits, some boulder beds and conglomerates. They are commonly well bedded, and some of them give clear indication of having fallen as a rain of volcanic debris into moving water. The deep-seated rocks, on the other hand, are relatively coarse-grained granites, porphyries, and diorites, many of them with large crystals of quartz and feldspar.

Cambrian rocks. The first-formed of the group of Lower Palaeozoic rocks, the Cambrian, are in utter contrast to the Pre-Cambrian igneous rocks on which they lie. They are sediments formed in a marine environment, and they demonstrate that after the ash and lava outbursts had died down and the intrusion of the granites had ceased there were widespread erosion and a drowning of the region beneath an advancing sea. The submergence was caused by a major large-scale sag of the earth's crust (called a geosyncline) that persisted throughout Lower Palaeozoic times. In the seas occupying the sag there accumulated the Cambrian, Ordovician, and Silurian rocks that in Pembrokeshire reach thicknesses exceeding 20,000 feet.

The Cambrian, in being the first transgressive deposits on the Pre-Cambrian foundation, are through much of their thickness sandy and gritty beds with some conglomeratic layers. They are particularly well displayed in the cliffs between St. David's and Newgale, and on the south shore of Whitesand Bay. At Porth Clais, Caerfai, and Caerbwdi the lower beds can be seen to rest unconformably on the Pre-Cambrian rocks, a conglomerate at their base containing derived pebbles of ash and granite. Higher beds of the Cambrian sequence are best seen at Porth-y-rhaw and Solva, the highest in Whitesand Bay and along the north-east coast of Ramsey Island, where they are finer-grained than the beds beneath and suggest deeper-water sedimentation. In full thickness the Cambrian rocks exceed 5,000 feet.

A particular feature of the Cambrian rocks is the appearance in them of fossils of a variety of kinds. Bivalved brachiopods (notably specimens of the genus *Lingulella*) crowd some of the bedding planes on Ramsey Island and in Whitesand Bay, and water-fleas and sponges have also been found; but the most notable fossils are the trilobites, distant kin of crabs and lobsters, whose segmented skeletons are abundant in some of the middle and upper Cambrian strata (specimens of the genus *Paradoxides* found in Solva Harbour may reach a foot in length).

Ordovician rocks. In general appearance many of the Ordovician rocks resemble the Cambrian, partly because they were deposited in the continuing environment of the Lower Palaeozoic geosyncline. They include sandstones and grits, and great thicknesses of shale; but they also include thick piles of volcanic ashes and lavas representing a second major pulse of igneous action—much later than the Pre-Cambrian Pebidian and Dimetian—that contributed to the rock-stuff of Pembrokeshire.

The volcanoes were intermittently active, the main centres of activity moving about as Ordovician times advanced. An early outburst was centred in the neighbourhood of the present Skomer[1], where accumulations of lavas, interbedded with normal marine sediments, are nearly 3,000 feet in thickness and can be followed from St. Ishmael's and Wooltack westwards to Grassholm and the Smalls. A little later, in mid-Ordovician times, a number of volcanoes became active, some near Treffgarne, where the large quarries are worked in lavas and ashes, some more powerful near Ramsey Island and Llanrhian, some in exceptional development about Strumble

---

[1] In traditional interpretation the Skomer rocks have long been regarded as early Ordovician in age. Recent work, however, strongly suggests that they are early Silurian.

Head where the forbidding cliffs are eroded in lavas poured one flow on another to thicknesses of thousands of feet. The highly local character of the volcanic outbursts is shown by reduction of the thickness of the Ramsey lavas from 1,400 feet on Ramsey Island to 500 feet at Llanrhian, and of the Strumble lavas from 3,600 feet on Pencaer to about 800 feet at Fishguard and about 400 feet in the Presely Hills.

The volcanoes were active in the Ordovician sea, the lavas building up the sea floor locally to heights above sea-level and the volcanic cones emerging as islands. But away from the volcanic centres deposition of normal marine sediments proceeded without interruption, and in many of them are to be found fossils in an abundance far exceeding the fossils of the Cambrian rocks. Lower beds in the Ordovician sequence yield many trilobites and brachiopods on Ramsey Island, where also graptolites may be found in some of the shales. Slightly younger mid-Ordovician shales are exceptionally rich in and near Abereiddi Bay, where tuning-fork graptolites lie in profusion on some of the bedding planes, and where trilobites also are not uncommon. At still higher horizons, in the upper beds of the Ordovician sequence, impure limestones (like the Castell limestone of Abereiddi) are interbedded with the shales and yield many brachiopods and trilobites—some of the limestones, like the Robeston Wathen and Shoalshook limestones, being composed in great part of shelly debris in which molluscs and corals are found with the usual brachiopods and trilobites.

Complementing the surface flows of volcanic lavas, deep-seated igneous rocks, formed when hot molten rock was forced into the sediments but failed to reach the surface before cooling, are represented by sills of dark-coloured dolerite that run more or less parallel to the bedding of the sediments but wedge out when followed for any distance. They are relatively resistant to erosion and commonly form headlands along the coast (Penclegyr, Penllechwen, St. David's Head), or monadnock hills and ridges inland (Carn Llidi, Penberi, Garn-Fawr, Garn-Folch): they are particularly abundant in the Presely Hills and contribute to their mountain form.

Silurian rocks. While there was no major change in the general geosynclinal environment at the close of Ordovician times, the Silurian rocks are conveniently distinguished from the underlying Ordovician by the occurrence of a break in sedimentation between them, brought about by uplift and some folding of the region that is now southern Pembrokeshire. As a consequence of the movements and of the exposure of the Ordovician rocks to erosion, there is strong Silurian overstep southwards; and while the Silurian base

PLATE 1. Pen-y-holt on the south coast

PLATE 2. Whitesand Bay and Ramsey Island

PLATE 3. Pen-yr-afr, near Cemais Head

PLATE 5. Eligug Stack

PLATE 4. Anticline at Saundersfoot

rests on strata high in the Ordovician sequence in outcrops between Narberth and Haverfordwest, it transgresses southwards on to very early Ordovician rocks at Freshwater East and on to Pre-Cambrian (all the Ordovician and Cambrian absent) between Talbenny and Llangwm.

Silurian rocks are less completely exposed than Ordovician. An outcrop diminishing from 4 miles wide follows the north coast from the Teifi estuary to Newport Bay and Dinas Head, where the rocks succeed the Ordovician conformably and consist of alternations of deep-water dark shales and gritty sandstones (greywackes), fossiliferous (with graptolites) in only a few bands, in a thickness of several thousand feet. They are separated in outcrop by 15 miles of Ordovician rocks from the Silurian belt running from Whitland and Narberth to Haverfordwest. In this belt the lithology of the rocks shows a radical change: they are mudstones and sandstones with impure limestones, fossiliferous with an abundance of brachiopods, trilobites, and corals. Well displayed in Haverfordwest and along the banks of the Western Cleddau, they reach a thickness of 5,000 feet as a series of shallow-water marine sediments contrasting with the relatively deep-water greywackes to the north.

Still farther south, in the small and isolated outcrops south of the coalfield, the Silurian sediments emphasise increasing proximity to the margins of the geosyncline. At Rosemarket, where they rest on Pre-Cambrian with great unconformity, and to the south, their lowest members were not deposited. At Marloes and Wooltack (where some of the beds are unusually coral-rich) they are about 3,000 feet thick, and rest on the Skomer volcanic rocks. They are reduced to about 280 feet at Freshwater West and to little more than 70 feet at Freshwater East, where they emerge as small inliers in Upper Palaeozoic terrain. The thinning is accompanied by the development of beach sands and shingle of a fluctuating Silurian shore virtually at the geosynclinal margin; and there are repeated discontinuities in the sequence of strata, and always a major unconformity at the base.

Thin lavas at Marloes and Wooltack, and probably the thick lavas of Skomer, are the only signs of volcanic activity in the Silurian rocks.

Late-Silurian folding. Towards the end of the Silurian period much of Britain, including Pembrokeshire, was subjected to intense earth-pressures, and the Lower Palaeozoic rocks were acutely deformed into folds of both large and small amplitude. In general structure northern Pembrokeshire may be regarded as an enormous but complex upfold with oldest (Pre-Cambrian) rocks in the heart about St. David's and Hayscastle, and with Silurian rocks on the flanks. The irregularities of minor folding superposed on the major structure are well illustrated by the discontinuous lenticular outcrops (preserved in narrow elongate downfolds) of Silurian rocks of the Whitland—Haverfordwest belt; and they are also to be seen, less spectacularly, in the repetition of beds on the coast between St. David's and Strumble Head.

The folding was accompanied by large-scale faulting, many fractures demonstrably breaking the continuity of outcrop where individual beds may be followed for any distance. It was also accompanied by great compression of the softer shaly beds in the Lower Palaeozoic rocks, upon many of which a close cleavage was imposed, with the development of the slates that formerly were of economic importance.

The present plateau surface of the region cuts across the folded rocks to reveal the complexity of the structures in a complexity of outcrop pattern; and details of the individual structures are magnificently exposed in the steep cliff-faces along the coast from Pen Cemais by St. David's Head to the north shores of St. Bride's Bay.

The end-Silurian earth-movements radically transformed the geography of Pembrokeshire. The Lower Palaeozoic geosyncline ceased to be, and the marine environment that had persisted for nearly 200 million years was replaced by a continental environment of folded mountain chains elevated above sea-level and exposed to intense subaerial erosion. In this transformation the Upper Palaeozoic rocks accumulated under conditions utterly different from the Lower, the first of them resting with great unconformity on the pared-down foundation.

The Old Red Sandstone. This everywhere follows the Silurian unconformably, as a mark of the discontinuity of sedimentary environments. It is composed of river and estuarine sands and muds whose detritus was transported from sources mainly to the north, under conditions not fully arid but sufficiently oxidising to allow a red colouration of the iron minerals to be pervasive. Many of the beds are ripple-marked and cross-laminated, and some of them show rain-spots and sun-cracking. Conglomerates interbedded with the finer sandstones are sometimes channelled and wedge-bedded, and point to deposition in stream-courses. Fossils include occasional plant fragments, rare specimens of fish-like ostracoderms, and (in the upper beds) ganoid fringe-finned fishes; but most of the beds are unfossiliferous. The general impression throughout is of deposition in great delta-fans or flood-plains fed by fluctuating rivers.

Geological Figures

Figure 1. Outline map of the geology of Pembrokeshire.

Figure 2. Reconstructions of the sedimentary history of the Palaeozoic rocks,

Figure 3. Section to illustrate compressive effects of earth-movements.

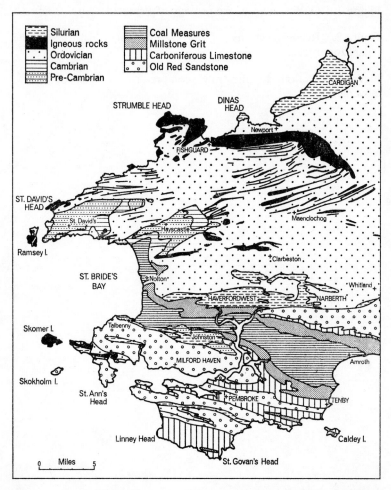

Fig. 1. *Simplified outline map of the geology of Pembrokeshire. No distinction is made between the volcanic tuffs and the granitic rocks of Pre-Cambrian age. Amongst the Ordovician igneous rocks are included the volcanic lavas, notably those running from Strumble Head eastwards into the Presely Hills, and the many intrusive doloritic dykes and sills*

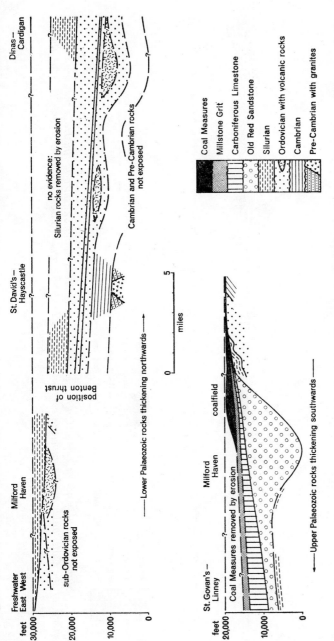

Fig. 2. *Diagrammatic reconstructions, much generalised and simplified, of the sedimentary history of the Palaeozoic rocks in Pembrokeshire. The upper section restores the relations as they may have been at the close of Silurian times, before the imposition of the main Caledonian movements: the lower section summarises the development of the Upper Palaeozoic rocks towards the close of Carboniferous times before the imposition of the Armorican earth-movements. In combination the two sections are designed to show the contrasted development of geological growth—the Lower Palaeozoic rocks being laid down in a major basin of sedimentation to the north of present Pembrokeshire, the Upper Palaeozoic rocks in a basin to the south*

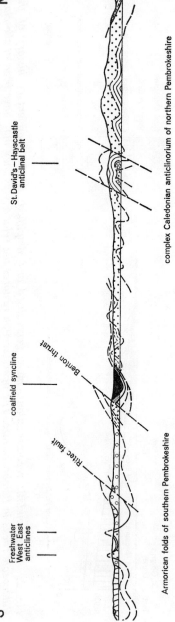

Fig. 3. *Simplified and generalised section from south to north across Pembrokeshire to illustrate the compressive effects of the Caledonian and Armorican earth-movements in the multiple folding and in the repetition of thrust faults*

S

N

Freshwater
West East
anticlines

coalfield syncline

St. David's—Hayscastle
anticlinal belt

Ritec fault

Benton thrust

Armorican folds of southern Pembrokeshire

complex Caledonian anticlinorium of northern Pembrokeshire

0   5
miles

Silurian
Ordovician
Cambrian
Pre-Cambrian with granites

Coal Measures
Millstone Grit
Carboniferous Limestone
Old Red Sandstone

The formation is some 4,000 feet thick in southern Pembroke-shire, where it is very well displayed along the coast from Old Castle Head to Stackpole Quay and from Freshwater West to West Angle Bay; but it reaches 15,000 feet in a deep depositional trough about Cosheston. Thereafter it thins rapidly northwards, and in the outcrops north of the coalfield it diminishes to nil between Narberth and Haverfordwest. There is clear indication of a northward approach to the margins of sedimentation, and of an emergent land area in the region of the present North Pembrokeshire oldland.

Hints of a southern sea are to be read into some of the uppermost beds of the formation in the outcrops south of Milford Haven, notably at West Angle, Freshwater West, Stackpole, Caldey, and especially Skrinkle: the usual sequence of red beds is interrupted by intercalations of grey calcareous layers, exceptional in the Old Red Sandstone in being fossiliferous with common specimens of brachio-pods (including spirifers), bivalves (mussels, pectens, rock-borers), snails, crustaceans, "worms", and crinoids, all forms typical of a shallow-water marine environment. The fossils match those found in the uppermost Devonian rocks of Devon, and they mark the first incursions of a sea in which the succeeding limestones were to be laid down.

Carboniferous Limestone. The rocks of the Carboniferous system look very different from the Old Red Sandstone, and in their earliest formation, the Carboniferous Limestone, they are in great contrast both in the character of the rocks of which they are formed and in the environment of sedimentation in which they accumulated. Neverthe-less, as the transitional Skrinkle beds show, a transformation from the non-marine Old Red geography to the marine Carboniferous was brought about by little more than a regional subsidence that allowed the seas of a contemporary Devon to advance and drown the river and delta-flats to the north: there were no major changes in the regional physique, which continued to be characterised by a rising land-mass to the north.

The rocks of the Carboniferous Limestone are usually so richly fossiliferous that they are limestones because they are composed, sometimes almost completely, of the skeletal debris of a great variety of marine organisms. The purity of some of the beds, virtually free of extraneous sand and mud, implies clear shallow waters of deposition, aerated by waves and hospitable particularly to crinoids, brachiopods, and corals. Crinoids are sometimes present in a profusion, through bed after bed in thicknesses of scores of feet, suggesting persistent crinoid gardens over many square miles of the contemporary sea floor; and corals, in colonies occasionally feet across or as crowded individuals strewn over bedding planes, are sometimes only to a degree less abundant. Seaweeds, of a kind secreting a limy skeleton, also periodically carpeted the sea floor with a multitude of biscuit-like or button-like growths. Brachiopods in gregarious multitudes crowd some shell beds in thicknesses of inches or feet. The multiplicity of shallow-water marine environments suggested by the fossils and their variable distribution provides a picture of conditions of sedimentation of the Carboniferous Limestone exceptional amongst Pembrokeshire rocks.

Other limestones, although contributing as limestones to the unity of the formation, are very different in origin. They are fine-grained lime muds formed in quiet undisturbed "lagoonal" waters, and oolites formed in agitated waters—both kinds in circumstances of high evaporation in very shallow seas, and of a consequent saturation and precipitation out of the sea-water of the lime as a chemical deposit. In conditions of such high salinity few organisms could survive, and these rocks are usually poorly fossiliferous. They alternate with the open-sea limestones rich in skeletal debris.

Details of change in the Carboniferous Limestone are abundantly revealed in the magnificent coastal sections and in the many inland quarries. The formation in unbroken sequence reaches thicknesses of 4,500 feet in the southernmost outcrops between Stackpole Head and Linney Head, where the cliffs are almost continuously in highly fossiliferous rocks. The thickness is reduced to about 2,000 feet between Tenby and Pembroke, where many of the beds are oolitic, and is further reduced to 1,500 feet near Carew and to 1,000 feet near Lawrenny. Still farther north discontinuities appear in the sequence and progressively become intensified: the outcrop running from Ludchurch towards Haverfordwest reveals only thin residual upper members of the formation, and at Haverfordwest the formation wedges out completely. The distribution of the outcrops of Carboniferous Limestone at the present time is thus a partial reflection of its original development in a sea whose floor sagged southwards from a shore lying not far north of the Haverfordwest—Narberth line.

Upper Carboniferous rocks. Limestone deposition was brought to an end by an influx of sands and muds from the land to the north, presumably following renewed uplift of the land and an intensification of erosion by rivers. The changed conditions of sedimentation were discouraging to the many kinds of organisms that flourished in the Lower Carboniferous seas, most of which migrated out of the area. The sandstones and shales that overlie the Carboniferous Limestone are grouped, the lower part as Millstone Grit, the upper part as Coal

Measures. The Millstone Grit contains a number of fossiliferous beds, of which goniatites and molluscs (but not corals and rarely brachiopods) are the signs, that indicate a continuing marine environment. The Coal Measures have only few and thin marine beds, restricted to the lower part, and were deposited as river and swamp sediments in which accumulations of peat beds gave rise to the formation of coal seams.

The Millstone Grit is poorly exposed. It forms a long outcrop to the south of the coalfield westwards as far as Johnston, but it is to be seen in any detail only on the foreshore of Tenby North Sands, where it is dominantly a sequence of folded and puckered shales perhaps 1,000 feet thick. To the north of the coalfield a more extended outcrop runs from Marros by Haverfordwest to Druidston Haven; but exposures are again poor, the thickness is reduced to about 500 feet, and only the upper part of the sequence is present, resting unconformably on thin residual Carboniferous Limestone or overstepping on to Ordovician rocks.

The Coal Measures are very well exposed along the coast from Monkstone Point by Saundersfoot to Amroth, and again along the coast of St. Bride's Bay from Talbenny to Newgale. They are, however, much affected by later earth-movements and are greatly deformed, so that it is difficult to determine the full sequence. The thickness is also difficult to estimate, but is of the order of 5,000 feet. The lower beds are predominantly shaly, and contain the anthracite coal seams (now no longer worked). The upper beds include thick sandstones. Fossil plant impressions are common on the bedding planes of some of the shales; and in the lower part of the sequence fresh-water bivalves form mussel bands; but in most of the beds fossils are rare, and only three or four thin marine bands are known.

In the southern outcrops there appears to be an unbroken sequence from the Millstone Grit into and through the Coal Measures; but in the 8 miles northwards from Talbenny by Nolton to Newgale the upper beds of the Coal Measures overstep the beds beneath, and in the northernmost outcrops they descend on to a foundation of Cambrian and Pre-Cambrian rocks. They are thus banked against a persistently rising floor of old rocks, and in their transgressive relations confirm the place of a northern land-mass as a controlling influence on sedimentation through Old Red Sandstone and Carboniferous times. It is thus probable that while southern Pembrokeshire received a pile of Upper Palaeozoic rocks that in total thickness reached 20,000 feet or more, northern Pembrokeshire had only a thin cover of upper Coal Measures resting directly on the thick Lower Palaeozoic rocks beneath.

Late-Carboniferous folding. After the deposition of the Coal Measures, a second major series of earth-movements affected Pembrokeshire. They were not so intense as those at the close of Silurian times, nor were their stresses aligned in exactly the same direction; but their effects were similar in the imposition of sharp folds and faults on the Upper Palaeozoic rocks (and no doubt on the already-deformed Lower Palaeozoic rocks also).

The downfold of the coalfield, in which the youngest rocks, the Coal Measures, are preserved, is the most considerable of these structures. It is continuous from St. Bride's Bay to Carmarthen Bay (beneath which it merges with the downfold of the South Wales coalfield). To the south of it there are downfolds of less amplitude, notably between Lydstep and Pembroke, and at Bosherston, in the heart of which Millstone Grit is still preserved. Between the downfolds are upfolds in which Old Red Sandstone and Lower Palaeozoic rocks come to the surface, notably along the Skomer line, and along the Castlemartin Corse axis eastwards from Freshwater West.

Many faults fracture the rocks, often in reticulate pattern. Two are particularly important. The Ritec fault, running from Tenby to Pembroke partly as a replacement of the limb of a fold, is a thrust on the surface of which the rocks to the south rode over the rocks to the north in a movement the vertical component of which was about 3,000 feet. The Benton fault is similar but larger: it also is a thrust, the ground to the south having been carried northwards over the downfold of the coalfield with sufficient movement to cause Pre-Cambrian rocks from the depths to override and come to rest upon Coal Measures.

The major product of the folding was a land-mass of corrugated mountain chains aligned slightly south of east and elevated into a zone of sustained subaerial erosion, whose pared-down subdued remnants formed the floor on which later sediments were deposited.

Mesozoic and Tertiary deposits. Few relics remain of the long interval of time, over 200 million years, that elapsed after the deposition and the folding of the Coal Measures. Red marls, sandstones, and coarse breccias, occupying pockets in the Carboniferous Limestone, are repeatedly seen along the coast between Tenby and Linney Head (notably in the Lydstep-Skrinkle cliffs and in Bullslaughter Bay). They belong to the New Red Sandstone and are probably of Triassic age. A more widespread red staining of the Carboniferous Limestone in southern Pembrokeshire may indicate a former cover of Trias like that still preserved in Glamorgan. But other signs of Mesozoic rocks are lacking, although it is not unlikely that Lias, and perhaps younger Mesozoic sediments, once overlay the Trias and extended inland.

A pocket near Flimston, several acres in area and some 45 feet deep, is unique in Pembrokeshire (as in South Wales) in containing very fine-grained white and mottled pipe-clays, with some inter-calated sandy beds, that rest on the local floor of Carboniferous Limestone. The deposit was formerly worked for pottery clay and abrasive powder, but the pits are now abandoned and overgrown and not much is to be seen. A dating of the deposits is difficult, for they have as yet yielded no fossils; in their main characteristics, however, they most closely resemble the early Tertiary (Eocene and especially Oligocene) rocks of southern England, of which they may be a remnant analogue.

Major landforms. The regional landscape in Pembrokeshire is manifestly only in minor degree a reflection of the geological structure. The great variety of rocks and the complexities of the folding are unrelated to the general plateau form, whose surface planes in-differently whatever lies beneath. This incongruity is to be seen everywhere, but is spectacular in southern Pembrokeshire, where the flat land surface cuts across the residual Triassic sediments and the Flimston pipe-clays.

The one agent of erosion capable of planing such a surface across complex geological structures is the sea, and a compelling inference is that Pembrokeshire (like much of Wales) has been uplifted from beneath the sea to expose what is in effect a surface of wave erosion, a former sea floor. The plateau must be later in age than the Flimston clays, and earlier than the glacial drifts that rest on it; and it has been insignificantly tilted by earth-movement since it was uplifted. It is thus probably of later Tertiary origin—that is, no more than a few million years old.

At the same time, the plateau rises in steps from heights of less than 200 feet to well-developed flats, nearer 600 feet, south of Strumble Head and north-east of Newport. There is thus a strong suggestion that the plateau is composite, and was uplifted in a series of pulses. The isolated hills that stand above the coastal low plateau—the Ridgeway hogback behind Tenby, Penberi and Carn Llidi near St. David's—are the relics of higher platforms in the plateau, fragmented by erosion. Well-marked steps in the plateau lie at about 600 feet, a little above 400 feet, and a little below 200 feet, many isolated hill summits being approximately concordant.

The indented and embayed coastal margins of the plateau carry remnants of a raised beach, a few feet above present high-water mark, that underlies the glacial deposits and defines in fragments the outline of the coast, scarcely different from the present outline, as it was before the arrival of the ice: the beach is well seen on Caldey, in

Manorbier and Swanlake Bays, at Freshwater West, in West Angle Bay, and at Porth Clais, where demonstrably the steep cliffs are relatively ancient.

In the Preglacial evolution of the coast by constant wave attack the differential resistance by the foundation rocks is expressed in the close relation between coastal form and geology: bays commonly are excavated in soft sediments, headlands stand out as tough grits and sandstone or as igneous rock—the fine correspondence being brought out particularly closely in almost every detail of the coast between Strumble Head and Caerbwdi.

Deposits of the Ice Age. There are few signs in the landscape of any intensity of glacial erosion in Pembrokeshire; and only one or two steep-sided hollows on the north face of the Presely Hills mildly hint at the cirques and the rock basins of North Wales. There is, however, impressive evidence of ice-movement across the area, partly in the exposure of ice-scratched rock surfaces (well developed on Carn Llidi at 500 feet, and in Whitesand Bay) but especially in the occurrence of a widespread veneer of boulder clay and fluvio-glacial gravels that reveal oscillations of climatic change during Pleistocene times. Along the north coast, notably in some of the bays between Strumble Head and Cardigan, there appear to be two layers of boulder clay, separated by intervening water-borne sand and gravel, that are clear indication of advance of the ice, and of a local melting during a mild interlude. Elsewhere such a tripartite division of the deposits is not so readily recognised, but drift to thicknesses of tens of feet, as stiff stony till or as well-washed melt-water sands and shingle, together with "head" and solifluvial loams, is commonly met in shallow diggings inland and is well seen in Whitesand Bay and in Milford Haven.

The pebbles in the boulder clay are often ice-scratched and polished and reveal their mode of transport. Many of them were derived from local sources, but a number are of rock types not found in place in Pembrokeshire: these include pebbles of granite matched by rock-in-place in Arran, Ailsa Craig, and Galloway in Scotland, and in the Isle of Man, and it is to be inferred that a regional ice-sheet that traversed Pembrokeshire from the north-west had its origins far to the north in the Clyde estuary and the Irish Sea. Very large boulders of such "foreign" erratics are scattered over the low ground of southern Pembrokeshire—one from Scotland lies in Bosherston village, another from North Wales overhangs the extremity of St. Govan's Head. Some of the drift deposits contain marine shells (mussels, cockles, tellens, whelks, periwinkles) dredged from the sea floor as the ice moved on to the land from the north-west.

The Irish Sea ice, fed from an extensive hinterland, underwent slow melting as the Ice Age came to an end. In one interpretation, it continued to impinge on the Pembrokeshire coast long after the small local glaciers of Welsh ice had disappeared. It formed a barrier to the free outflow of the rivers into Cardigan Bay and St. George's Channel, and dammed up temporary lakes in the river valleys along the north and west coasts. The pattern of these lakes may still be recognised, although they were drained when the Irish Sea ice finally melted, by the marshy flats of their lake floor sediments, notably the sediments of "Lake Maenorowen" south-west of Fishguard. They are also defined by the abandoned gaps through which overspill from the temporary lakes found its way to the sea: the Gwaun valley, now dry at its north-eastern limit, drained "Lake Nevern" into Fishguard Bay; the Jordanston channel drained "Lake Maenorowen" into the Cleddau; Cwmyreglwys briefly took over from the Gwaun valley as a late spillway from "Lake Nevern" and separated Dinas "Island" from the mainland; Barry "Island" between Porthgain and Abereiddi matches Dinas "Island" in being similarly cut off by an abandoned spillway; Dale Roads formed the exit of a spillway at one stage from St. Bride's Haven 3 miles to the north, and at another stage from Westdale Bay a mile to the west; and the Wooltack peninsula and the Neck of Skomer are isolated by similar overflow channels.

In an alternative interpretation, ice-dammed lakes at best had a brief life; and the anomalous drainage channels, now dry, are not to be regarded as lake outlets but as subglacial melt-water courses temporarily occupied under a waning ice cover and abandoned when the ice finally melted.

Temporary amelioration of climate during the Ice Age is indicated by cave deposits, notably in Hoyle's Mouth near Tenby and on Caldey, that have yielded an abundance of bones of "cold" animals including mammoth, reindeer, Irish elk, woolly rhino, cave bear, hyena, and cave lion.

Postglacial deposits. The world-wide rise in sea-level that followed the melting of the ice at the close of the Ice Age about 12,000 years ago is marked in Pembrokeshire (as elsewhere in north-western Europe) by the drowned peats and associated sediments seen in many of the bays (Amroth, Saundersfoot, Lydstep, Manorbier, Freshwater East, Freshwater West, St. Bride's, Whitesand). They consist of a matt of roots, twigs, and branches of trees (oak, alder, birch, hazel), sometimes with boles in position of growth, that accumulated above tide-level but are now found covered by beach sand. The associated marsh sediments contain fresh-water snails and bivalves, and Neolithic flints have been found under the peat at a number of localities.

The drowning of the coast also converted the river mouths into estuaries—minor in Newport Bay and Solva Harbour, major in the ria of Milford Haven and its tributaries.

3

The Fauna of the Park

by R. M. LOCKLEY

Bird life. Nowhere in England and Wales is there a richer sea-bird life than along the Pembrokeshire coast, for which reason it is famous with ornithologists. The little island of Grassholm has one of the largest colonies of gannets in the world; there are today above 15,000 nests of this fine goose-sized bird (Plate 7), which, allowing for two adults, one nestling, and at least one immature bird to each pair, makes a total of over 60,000 gannets by the middle of summer.

But Grassholm is only 22 acres, rock-bound, waterless, lying in fierce tide-races 12 miles offshore, difficult of access except in the calmest weather. Skomer, 722 acres, is far more accessible, only a short passage from the boat-beach of Martin's Haven which lies under the beautiful headland (the Deer Park) above Jack Sound; all within the National Park, and well worth at least a day visit.

About 60 years ago Skomer was farmed, but today the island is a national nature reserve (managed by the West Wales Naturalists' Trust) unique for its archaeological, botanical, and, above all, ornithological interest. It contains huge colonies of Manx shearwaters, thousands of guillemots, razorbills, puffins, and gulls, and smaller numbers of oystercatchers, shags, cormorants, fulmar petrels, and rock-pipits. Wheatears, meadow-pipits, and other small birds also breed, and the short-eared owl nests each year, feeding largely on the insular vole, mouse, and shrews. Nature is allowed a free hand, but there is a resident warden to advise visitors and check abuses; these may come from over-eager naturalists disturbing nesting birds, or from some of the larger gulls killing too many of the smaller sea-birds, or taking their eggs.

To study those extraordinary birds, the shearwaters, it is best to remain at night, for this little black-and-white albatross is strictly nocturnal on its return to the burrow in which it lays its single white egg. Both sexes incubate over 7 weeks and there is a protracted period of another 70 days before the chick leaves the hidden nest. It is a marvellous experience to be abroad on Skomer or Skokholm on a dark, preferably stormy, midnight in early summer. Tens of thousands of shearwaters come screaming home from wandering at sea, to visit mate or chick which has remained perfectly silent all day

17

deep underground. Probably at least 100,000 pairs breed at Skomer, and another 35,000 pairs on the nearby island of Skokholm (242 acres). Yet all day long and until the first flocks gather offshore at sunset not a single live shearwater appears above the soil containing the world's largest concentration of this species!

On the other hand, the amusing pompous-looking puffin with the parrot bill (Plate 6) is diurnal. It likes to parade sociably along the island cliff-tops on a sunny afternoon, and is delightfully tame. A few thousands nest on Skomer and Skokholm. On arrival in April the mated puffins spring-clean the rabbit-burrow in which the single egg is laid. Later the adults bring beakloads of fresh sprats and sand-eels to feed raw to the black downy ball of their precocious chick. It fattens rapidly; but like the shearwater chick, it is finally abandoned by the adults which depart in August. Fledgeling puffin and shearwater survive well on their reserve of fat which carries them over the difficult period of getting away to sea (by night) and migrating alone. Eventually, guided only by a miraculous inborn sense of direction, they join up with the adults thousands of miles away, the shearwater wintering off the coast of South America, and the puffin often reaching the coast of North America.

Unique too is the colony of some 1,000 pairs of that charming bird the storm-petrel, the Mother Carey's Chicken of the sailor, on Skokholm, another reserve maintained by the West Wales Naturalists' Trust, where intensive natural history studies have been carried out ever since it was made the first British bird observatory in 1933.

Large colonies of gulls breed on many of the cliffs in the Park and abundantly on the islands: thousands of herring-gulls, hundreds of lesser black-backed gulls, and fewer great black-backed gulls. The charming inoffensive kittiwake gulls nest on many steep cliffs. Fulmar petrels, extending their range, breed here and there on high cliffs. Should the weather be too rough for a visit to an island, all these birds can be seen nesting in southern Pembrokeshire—at Eligug Stack (Plate 5) and the cliffs opposite. The fantastic sheer pillars of these Stacks are covered with nesting guillemots and razor-bills within a stone's throw of where your car is parked.

Of the larger land-birds the buzzard (Plate 8) is as numerous as the common kestrel, a splendid sight as it soars like a miniature eagle on broad pinions in the air currents of the shore, and upon thermals of warm air inland. It nests freely on cliff or in trees.

At one time there were up to 35 pairs of peregrine falcons along this coast, common enough for some eyries to be all too accessible. But as everywhere today this noble bird has declined in number, less, it is believed, because of robbery of eyries by falconers than through chemical poisons (used as pesticides on the land) being absorbed with the bodies of birds and small mammals, its prey. A few peregrines still survive, and these wander the length of the National Park coast out of the nesting season.

Its present scarcity may have helped the increase of rock doves in the Park. Large flights of these, diluted by gone-wild multi-coloured homing pigeons (originally bred from the true-blue wild rock-dove stock) and their progeny, haunt caves and overhanging cliffs where they roost and interbreed. Another pigeon which has increased in the Park is the pretty collared dove—one of the largest colonies of this recent immigrant to Britain is at St. David's. Some stock doves also breed.

Vanished from its last English haunts, and now rare in Scotland, the chough, that handsome glossy blue-black crow with the scarlet bill and legs, still holds its own on the Park cliffs. Possibly 30–40 pairs nest, most of them in inaccessible cave sites. The quiet observer can see them at fairly close quarters as they probe the grass with curved beak or loop along in graceful flight with splayed wings.

More numerous, and haunting the whole steep coastline, the raven has long established its territories from one end of the Park to the other, with one or more pairs on each of the islands and a few pairs inland. In late summer the young birds from these nests may form large flocks, occasionally up to 100 strong, which roost communally upon some safe crag or mountainside. They may feed in numbers on dead sheep, at abattoir or rubbish dump, useful scavengers but mistrusted by farmers who are apt to blame them, albeit unfairly, for losses of sheep and lambs.

Pembrokeshire is less remarkable than many a more sheltered southern English county for the number of common smaller nesting species. But open country species such as stonechat, yellowhammer, linnet, grasshopper warbler, are plentiful; a list of common birds not mentioned in the text is given below. What would be too long to enumerate here is the full list of rare birds which have been recorded in the Park, chiefly by observation and ringing at Skokholm Bird Observatory in the last 40 years: a list longer than that of any other county in Wales, and containing some species very rarely recorded anywhere in the British Isles.

The estuarine part of the Park, the upper reaches of Milford Haven, and the sandy tidal waters of the county, are visited by flocks, large and small, of waders and ducks too numerous to describe here. These are chiefly seen out of the breeding season, but a few handsome shelducks remain to nest, and so do herons. Mallard inhabit the whole coast, often hatching their ducklings in strange sites, such as steep cliffside nests. The many farm irrigation reservoirs provide good points for watching water-birds.

Leaving the north coast and wandering inland through the Gwaun valley and Presely Hills portion of the Park brings a somewhat gentler ornithological scene of woodland and moorland birds. Buzzards, owls, kestrels, and ravens there are still, and in the hanging woods and leafy lanes the flash of the hunting sparrowhawk may be noted. The native trees of sessile oak, ash, sycamore, and hazel provide cover for singing warblers: garden, willow, and wood warblers, blackcap, chiffchaff, and perhaps the rare redstart and nightjar. Beside the fast-flowing streams where salmon and sewin (sea-trout) run, the dipper is resident, building its moss nest under bridge or hanging tree-root, hunting its insect and caddis-worm food as it walks submerged along the pebbly water-course. Its thin song blends with the rippling call of another resident, the beautiful grey wagtail, whose rich yellow breast and graceful tail flashes past gaudy mimulus and kingcup—a pleasing sight. There are a few kingfishers; and sedgewarbler and reed-bunting are nesting in every marshy covert.

On the heights of Presely we meet again the land-birds of the bare windswept islands and coast: meadow-pipits and skylarks abound; wheatears nest where the rocky cairns and long stone dykes protrude. Characteristic sound of the moorland scene is the melodious call of the curlew, which also nests freely in damp lowland meadows. Where there are bushes and new forestry plantations whinchats nest; and with luck you may see merlin, ring-ouzel, and woodlark.

Common species not mentioned above

Residents: Blackbird, Bullfinch, Chaffinch, Carrion Crow, Dunnock, Goldcrest, Goldfinch, Greenfinch, Jackdaw, Jay, Lapwing, Magpie, Moorhen, Nuthatch, Owls (Barn, Little, Tawny), Pheasant, Ring-dove, Robin, Rook, Common Snipe, House Sparrow, Starling, Mute Swan, Thistlesand, Song Thrushes, Tits (Blue, Coal, Great, Long-tailed, Marsh), Tree-creeper, Pied Wagtail, Woodpeckers (Green, Great Spotted), Wren.

Summer visitors nesting: Cuckoo, Spotted Flycatcher, House and Sand Martins, Swallow, Swift, Whitethroat. (Scarce as breeding birds are Black-headed Gull, Partridge, Tree-Pipit, Ringed Plover, Lesser Redpoll, Redshank, Common Sandpiper, Willow Tit.)

Common non-breeding and winter visitors: Brambling, Coot, Red-throated Diver, Ducks (various), Fieldfare, Little Grebe, Golden Plover, Redwing, Jack Simple, Waders (various), Woodcock.

Mammals. Seals are the largest and most interesting of the mammals of the National Park. Fortunately they can be watched at almost any point along the coast, as they fish over high tide, and bask and laze on the rocks over low water (Plate 9). Save for the big herds in Scotland and the Farne Islands off Northumberland, Pembrokeshire may be said to possess the largest breeding group of the grey seal (*Halichoerus grypus*) in the British Isles. Undoubtedly this is due chiefly to long protection at its main nurseries of Ramsey Island, where about 200 pups are born annually, and Skomer, which produces 50–60 pups each autumn. In addition the beaches hidden at the back of the numerous and mostly inaccessible caves and cover under the mainland cliffs of the Park produce an average of another 100 pups. These round figures are derived from a recent 10-year seal-marking survey and count by members of the West Wales Naturalists' Trust. Marking of individual pups has proved that some wander from Pembrokeshire and, within a few months of birth, swim to the west of Ireland, or to Brittany; one has even reached Spain.

No deer are now found in the Park. The next largest land mammals are the fox and badger, which breed in dens and sets throughout Park territory. They may be encountered occasionally in daylight, by the early riser or late stroller in the wilder places.

Rabbits, scarcer since myxomatosis, are present in small colonies here and there. The hare, once virtually extinct, is rare but may soon increase, for it has been reintroduced on some estates. Rabbits abound on the islands of Ramsey, Skokholm, and Skomer. Of these, Skomer has a unique subspecies (*skomerensis*) of the common bank vole—larger, more tawny, and tamer than the mainland race; and there are also long-tailed field mouse and common and pigmy shrews on this national nature reserve.

Other mammals found commonly within the Park are common, pigmy, and water shrews, mole, hedgehog, stoat, weasel, grey squirrel, brown rat, house mouse, long-tailed field (wood) mouse, and field, bank, and water voles. Pipistrelle and long-eared bats are numerous, and in caves and quarries, especially in the limestone of the southern cliffs, great and lesser horse-shoe bats form considerable colonies.

Rarely seen are the polecat, mink (escaped from fur-farms and now breeding wild), and red squirrels (a few may possibly survive in the wooded Daugleddau region).

At sea, the common porpoise is frequently seen close inshore. Dolphins of several species have been recorded; and more rarely, pilot and other whales.

4

Flora and Vegetation

by T. A. WARREN DAVIS

MUCH of the National Park is fertile and intensively cultivated farmland, but it includes wide stretches of open moorland, heath, and bog on the Presely Hills. Other natural and semi-natural plant communities are well represented on steep hillsides with scrub or bracken (*Pteridium aquilinum*), woodland, lowland bogs, marshes in the river and stream valleys, cliffs, sand-dunes, and estuarine saltmarshes. The diversity of rock formations and soils gives rise to local differences in the floras of the major communities. A mild climate gives a long growing season: the geographical elements in the flora best represented are the oceanic-southern, the Lusitanian or oceanic-west European, and the continental-southern. Northern elements are more numerous than continental, while arctic and alpine elements are represented by a single arctic-alpine species, roseroot (*Sedum rosea*), which grows on a cliff of basic rock near the St. David's Head coastguard station.

Visitors to the county are introduced to its plant life at the roadside. Except where recent roadworks have changed the character of main roads, most roads and lanes run between high earth-and-stone banks which carry a rich flora and are crowned by bushes and trees: they are beautiful at all seasons. In early spring, lesser celandines (*Ranunculus ficaria*) and locally snowdrops (*Galanthus nivalis*) make a display, soon joined by a blaze of dandelions (*Taraxacum officinale*) along the hedge-bottoms, primroses (*Primula vulgaris*), the pink variety being by no means rare, greater stitchwort (*Stellaria holostea*), and, chiefly near the coast, scurvy grass (*Cochlearia officinalis*). In late April and May taller plants dominate the hedges, notably cow parsley (*Anthriscus sylvestris*) and red campion (*Silene dioica*), often with a delightful mingling of their white and pink flowers. For contrast there may be patches of deep blue germander speedwell (*Veronica chamaedrys*) where growth is not too tall. On the hedge-tops gorse is in flower sporadically all through the winter and is well out by mid-March when blackthorn (*Prunus spinosa*) comes into blossom. The local but not uncommon wild cherry (*Prunus cerasus*) is out in April, followed in May by

22

hawthorn (*Crataegus monogyna*) and in June and July by dog roses (*Rosa* spp.) and honeysuckle (*Lonicera periclymenum*). At this time the hedge-banks are draped with sorrel (*Rumex acestosa*), rough chervil (*Chaerophyllum temulentum*), hogweed (*Heracleum sphondylium*), the yellow dandelion-like flowers of the ubiquitous cat's-ear (*Hypochaeris radicata*), hawksbeard (*Crepis capillaris*), rough hawkbit (*Leontodon hispidus*), and tall grasses such as cocksfoot (*Dactylis glomerata*) and oat grass (*Arrhenatherum elatius*). In the moorland districts of northern Pembrokeshire the banks are frequently clothed with the beautiful flowering heads of tufted and wavy hair-grass (*Deschampsia cespitosa* and *D. flexuosa*). Later in the summer, flowers in mass are less general and those that make a display are, at least at the wayside, rather local: they include field scabious (*Knautia arvensis*) and, in damp hedge-bottoms, meadow-sweet (*Filipendula ulmaris*), purple loosestrife (*Lythrum salicaria*), and hemp agrimony (*Eupatorium cannabinum*), so attractive to butterflies. In autumn the hedges are adorned by the scarlet fruits of hawthorn, dog roses, honeysuckle, and black bryony (*Tamus communis*), and ferns of several kinds, some of which are green all winter.

Though modern methods of hedge and verge trimming are often criticised and it is to be regretted that a stretch of road is sometimes cut when the flowers are at their best, the machines can now be adjusted so as to avoid too close cutting. On the credit side, chemical sprays are not used in the county. Some of the verges created by road improvements during the past 20 years have been colonised profusely by early purple orchids (*Orchis mascula*) which are at their best in May. A few of these, by an arrangement with the county surveyor, are not cut while in flower and developing seed; they are marked by white posts bearing the letters NR, as roadside nature reserves, by the West Wales Naturalists' Trust. A few other uncommon and particularly attractive species are similarly marked. These protected areas are only an infinitesimal part of the beautiful hedges and verges in the National Park.

The Presely region of the Park is predominantly moorland and heath with heather or ling (*Calluna vulgaris*) covering much of the hills except in flushes and bogs, associated with much bilberry (*Vaccinium myrtillus*), heath rush (*Juncus squarrosus*), a little bell-heather (*Erica cinerea*), and, in many places, western gorse (*Ulex gallii*). There are rather few species all characteristic of moorland heaths in general. Western gorse, with flowers of a deeper golden yellow than those of common gorse, blooms in late summer and autumn; where it grows with purple heather the moors are particularly beautiful at that time. The hills are grazed by sheep and ponies and sometimes by cattle; the bilberry is cropped closest so that fruit is plentiful only on banks and the less accessible places. There is more variety in the flora of bogs and flushes, for though all are acid and peaty, the degree of acidity and the richness in bases of the ground water are not uniform. The wetter parts are a mosaic of hummocks and depressions covered by *Sphagnum* mosses. Common plants include bog asphodel (*Narthecium ossifragum*) in abundance, equally beautiful in July and August with spikes of yellow flowers and later with stems and capsules a rich orange-brown; cotton sedge (*Eriophorum angustifolium*) with white cottony tassels; round-leaved sundew (*Drosera rotundifolia*) in patches of *Sphagnum;* bog St. John's wort (*Hypericum elodes*) with pale velvety leaves; and the delicate ivy-leaved bell-flower (*Wahlenbergia hederifolia*). Among interesting local or rare plants are hare's-tail cotton sedge (*Eriophorum vaginatum*), bog myrtle (*Myrica gale*), cranberry (*Vaccinium oxycoccos*), common and western butterwort (*Pinguicula vulgaris* and *P. lusitanica*), long-leaved sundew (*Drosera intermedia*), white beak-rush (*Rhynchospora alba*), bog orchid (*Hammarbya paludosa*), and marsh clubmoss (*Lycopodium inundatum*). In dry heath, stag's-horn and fir clubmoss (*L. clavatum* and *L. selago*) occur sparingly.

In the St. David's district also there is much moorland on Dowrog Moor and Tretio Common and on Trefeiddan and other moors. The heath and bog vegetation is broadly like that of Presely but there are differences, especially among the local and uncommon plants. Orchids are well represented by five species, the common marsh orchid (*Dactylorhiza praetermissa*), dwarf purple orchid (*D. purpurella*), heath spotted orchid (*D. maculata* ssp. *ericetorum*), twayblade (*Listera ovata*), and lesser butterfly orchid (*Platanthera bifolia*). There are a few rare plants, notably waved St. John's wort (*Hypericum undulatum*) and *Cicendia filiformis*, a tiny plant of the gentian family with yellow flowers which open in sunshine in July and August. There are large pools of permanent water on Dowrog and Trefeiddan, and on Dowrog smaller but deeper pools in old clay pits. The area of open water on the large pools is now very small as aquatic vegetation extends over them. The principal plants are bogbean (*Menyanthes trifoliata*) and water horsetail (*Equisetum fluviatile*), the former, in May and early June, creating a beautiful picture with sheets of pinkish-white flowers. Interesting aquatic plants in some of the pools are pillwort (*Pilularia globulifera*), lesser bladderwort (*Utricularia minor*), and the very rare floating water plantain (*Luronium natans*). Commoner plants include water plantain

(*Alisma plantago-aquatica*), lesser water plantain (*Baldellia ranunculoides*), and bog St. John's wort.

There are 180 miles of rocky coast with cliffs mostly about 100 feet high, but in parts of northern Pembrokeshire up to 400 and even 500 feet. They are seen at their best in spring and early summer when, in many places, natural rock gardens are created by the profusion of lovely flowers. The following, more or less in order of their coming into flower, provide a succession from March to June: gorse, scurvy grass, sea campion (*Silene maritima*), thrift (*Armeria maritima*), kidney vetch (*Anthyllis vulneraria*), spring squill (*Scilla verna*), bird's-foot trefoil (*Lotus corniculatus*), ox-eye daisy (*Chrysanthemum leucanthemum*), sheep's bit (*Jasione montana*), and, locally, sheets of cowslips (*Primula veris*) on precipitous grassy slopes. Later in the summer scentless mayweed (*Tripleurospermum maritimum* ssp. *maritimum*) and rock samphire (*Crithmum maritimum*), with fleshy leaves and yellowish umbels, are conspicuous. On the limestone cliffs of southern Pembrokeshire other later-flowering plants are added, notably greater knapweed (*Centaurea scapiosa*), with large reddish-purple heads in June and July, and golden samphire (*Inula crithmoides*) and rock sea lavender (*Limonium binervosum*) in July and August. The sea lavender occurs locally on other rocks. Some of the above-mentioned plants are not restricted to sea cliffs but all are tolerant of wind and salt spray. Two ferns deserve special mention though they are not rare. Sea spleenwort (*Asplenium marinum*) is strictly maritime and most often grows in inaccessible places beneath an overhang where seepage just darkens the rock, so that unless specially sought it may be overlooked, although it occurs all round the coast. Royal fern (*Osmunda regalis*) is usually associated with marshes and bogs but grows in several places on cliffs from St. Bride's Bay to Cemais Head, favouring more obvious seepage lines on the cliff face and moist precipitous cliff slopes. On the islands off the Pembrokeshire coast, particularly Skokholm, Skomer, and Ramsey, flowers of the cliff spread upwards on to the slopes above and even on to level ground with the result that, on the west coast of Skomer for instance, thrift forms a sward several acres in extent, a wonderful sight at the height of its flowering in May and early June. On the islands it is not only maritime plants that give displays surpassing their mainland achievements. Great sheets of bluebells, interspersed with patches of very robust and richly coloured red campion, cover areas that will later have a blanket of bracken. On cliff ledges in the less exposed parts, lesser celandines and primroses abound. One rather common maritime plant, tree-mallow (*Lavatera arborea*), has its main habitat on offshore stacks, especially those with colonies of

gulls or auks, Eligug Stack at Flimston being an example. It is
evidently susceptible to browsing by rabbits but extremely tolerant
of high concentrations of guano.

A few plants to be found on Pembrokeshire cliffs occur in few
other localities in Britain. Prostrate broom (*Sarothamnus scoparius*
ssp. *maritimus*) differs from common broom (ssp. *scoparius*) in its
spreading or prostrate habit, often with stems tightly pressed to a
rock face or the ground. It grows in a number of places between
St. Ann's and Cemais Heads, most frequently on the Dale and
Marloes cliffs, on precipitous rock faces and with gorse and blackthorn on the cliff-top. Hairy greenweed (*Genista pilosa*) occurs at
St. David's Head and a few other stations in the vicinity and near
Strumble Head. It is a dwarf replica of prostrate broom, and both
make a striking display in May and early June. Perennial centaury
(*Centaurium portense*) (Plate 11) is a beautiful little plant which
grows in tufts bearing a mass of bright pink flowers from late June to
August, often with heather above cliffs but also on dunes. In Britain
it is known only near Newport and in west Cornwall. Two species of
rock sea lavender each have only one station in Ireland and one in
Pembrokeshire: *Limonium paradoxum* grows on basic rock at St.
David's Head and *L. transwallianum* is plentiful over a limited area
at Giltar Point.

There are sand-dunes in most of the southern Pembrokeshire
bays. The burrows between Tenby and Penally and those at Freshwater West are the most extensive. The vegetation is typical of west
coast dunes with marram grass (*Ammophila arenaria*) dominating the
fore-dunes and all unstable areas. Much of Tenby Burrows is a golf
course and a large area is now covered in dense sea buckthorn
(*Hippophae rhamnoides*) introduced to fix the sand in 1930; in
consequence some of the most attractive plants have been lost. A
plant that in Pembrokeshire grows only in this dune system is the
sharp rush (*Juncus acutus*), in big prickly clumps of dark green stems.
In the Freshwater West dunes are good slacks that are now probably
the only stations in the county in which the marsh helleborine
(*Epipactis palustris*) still occurs. Another locality with interesting
dune systems is at Stackpole, with burrows in Barafundle Bay, an
area of dunes behind limestone cliffs in Stackpole Warren and
actively growing dunes at Broad Haven, Bosherston. In northern
Pembrokeshire there are dunes at Whitesand Bay, St. David's,
Newport Sands (another golf course), and on the Teifi estuary. Some
of the more attractive plants to be seen on dunes are sea holly
(*Eryngium maritimum*), a bushy plant with spiny blue-green leaves
and blue flower heads, burnet rose (*Rosa pimpinellifolia*), sea bind-

PLATE 6. Puffins

PLATE 7. Gannet on Grassholm

PLATE 8. Young buzzards

PLATE 9.   Baby seal on Skomer

PLATE 11.   Newport centaury (*Centaurium portense*)

PLATE 10.   Tenby daffodil (*Narcissus obvallaris*)

PLATE 12. The Peacock Worm (*Sabella pavonina*) opens its crown of tentacles as the tide returns across the muddy or sandy flat

PLATE 13. The Masked Crab (*Corystes cassivelaunus*) that lives in sand

PLATE 14. The Presely Hills from Mynydd Bach

PLATE 15. Looking towards Mynydd Caregog on the Presely Hills, whence the bluestones were taken to Stonehenge

weed (*Calystegia soldanella*), carline thistle (*Carlina vulgaris*), ploughman's spikenard (*Inula conyza*), blue fleabane (*Erigeron acer*), sea pansy (*Viola tricolor* ssp. *curtisii*), the beautiful pyramidal orchid (*Anacamptis pyramidalis*), and, in one or two places, the bee orchid (*Ophrys apifera*).

Milford Haven has many areas of salt-marsh in the estuaries of its streams and rivers. The best is the Gann estuary, near Dale, where all stages of succession from seashore to land never reached by the highest tides are well represented. Most of the salt-marsh plants flower in mass and so make an impact. In spring the white long-leaved scurvy grass (*Cochlearia anglica*) is the first to flower. Next comes thrift, here later than on cliffs, followed in June by sea meadow grass (*Puccinellia maritima*) and in July by sea aster (*Aster tripolium*), sea purslane (*Halimione portulacoides*) with mealy grey leaves and yellowish fluffy flowers, and lax-flowered sea lavender (*Limonium humile*), so abundant here that the prevailing colour of many acres of salting is a soft blue-purple. The sea lavender is frequent throughout Milford Haven but does not occure elsewhere in the county. On banks of muddy sand covered at high water of all tides there are large patches of glasswort (*Salicornia* spp.), low, much-branched plants with fleshy green articulated stems. There are also narrow belts of salt-marsh in northern Pembrokeshire on the estuaries of the Nevern and Teifi.

During the second World War, cord grass (*Spartina* × *townsendii*) was introduced in the estuary of the Carew river whence it rapidly spread throughout Milford Haven so that it now blankets large areas. By 1952 aerial photographs showed that it had already dominated 25 acres in the Haven. It was first found on the Gann in 1950 and there now occupies several acres to the exclusion of most other plants, while clumps and smaller patches are scattered all over the saltings. It is also established on the Teifi estuary where its origin and time of arrival are not known. Like sea buckthorn it is an aggressive plant: it threatens to displace much of the native salt-marsh flora, and no practical method of control has yet been found.

The area of natural or semi-natural woodland in the National Park is not great and is unfortunately diminishing and being replaced by conifer plantations, but there are still pleasant woods of durmast oak (*Quercus petraea*), usually on steep and sometimes rocky hillsides, in the Gwaun valley and on the banks of the river Cleddau. As a rule the trees are not large since they are mostly grown from coppice after felling during either of the World Wars. They are, nevertheless, natural oakwoods in character with a typical flora and they provide habitats for woodland animals of all classes. Their contribution to the landscape is of great importance; indeed the Gwaun valley is rightly renowned for its beauty. Within the woods the ground is often densely carpeted with the great wood-rush (*Luzula sylvatica*), but where this is not so, such attractive woodland plants as lesser celandines, primroses, wood anemones (*Anemone nemorosa*), and bluebells may be abundant. Later in the year the very local cow-wheat (*Melampyrum pratense*), a semi-parasite on the roots of grasses, makes a display of yellow flowers in large patches.

Steep hillsides with bracken or scrub or gorse, blackthorn and hawthorn, are a feature of Pembrokeshire scenery and when the shrubs are in flower they may dominate it. The marshy bottoms of stream valleys can also be arresting with great patches of yellow flags (*Iris pseudacorus*) and hemlock water dropwort (*Oenanthe crocata*) in May and June, followed by meadowsweet, purple loosestrife, and hemp agrimony. The banks of the streams are often lined with sallow (*Salix cinerea* ssp. *atrocinerea*) and perhaps alder (*Alnus glutinosa*): their catkins, out from late February, are harbingers of spring.

The Tenby daffodil (*Narcissus obvallaris*) (Plate 10) has aroused interest for more than 150 years on account of the mystery of its origin and the beauty of its flowers, which are out before the end of February. It may well be indigenous in West Wales since legends that it was brought to Pembrokeshire from the Continent are discounted by the fact that it is not known as a native species anywhere in Europe. It was abundant in fields around Tenby until in the nineteenth century it became an object of trade, with the result that the country was scoured for the bulbs. A letter from a local botanist, J. E. Arnett, quoted by C. T. Vachell (*Transactions of the Cardiff Naturalists' Society, 1893–94*), records that up to 1885 there was a steady trade and that "about half a million bulbs were sent to London in the course of two years". By 1893 few Tenby daffodils remained. Increasing use of the plough has almost if not quite exterminated any that survived, though there are a few records as recent as the 1950s which may refer to plants still growing in traditional fields. It is, however, to be seen in many places in the National Park on roadside hedge-banks near dwellings or ruins, in pastures close to farmsteads, and in woods near large country houses, with every indication that it is thoroughly naturalised.

A by-law of Pembrokeshire County Council prohibits the uprooting of wild plants at the roadside and wherever the public have access. Taking wild plants in order to try to grow them in a garden is a practice to be deplored. They seldom survive. Two that are sometimes taken by plant-hunters are thrift and rock sea lavender, both of which have very deep tap roots which penetrate several feet into rock fissures so that it is not possible to pull them out with their roots; it is unlikely that they would grow even if they could be taken with roots. People do not always realise that picking flowers, especially on a large scale for sale, can do great harm. In some parts of Britain, so common a plant as the primrose has become rare as a result of excessive gathering of the flowers. Wild flowers should be left where they grow so that other people can enjoy their beauty and so that their seed may be allowed to ripen. A Wild Plants Protection Bill has been drafted and there is hope that it will be introduced in Parliament. Amongst other clauses it will give special protection to certain rare species and will prohibit the gathering of wild flowers for sale.

No Flora has been published for Pembrokeshire but one is being prepared by T. A. Warren Davis. The West Wales Naturalists' Trust has published *Plants of Pembrokeshire*, by the same author, and there have been a number of plant lists, mostly for restricted localities. The most comprehensive is the late Mrs. F. L. Rees's *List of Pembroke-shire Plants* (West Wales Field Society, 1950); it covers chiefly Tenby and southern Pembrokeshire but includes records from other localities, some made by the late Bertram Lloyd, a frequent visitor to the county in the 1920s and 1930s. A long list of his records appeared in the *North-Western Naturalists* (1948). *A Contribution to the Flora of the St. David's Peninsula*, by the late Dr. C. L. Walton (W.W.F.S., 1951), includes published records, notably those of W. R. Linton and E. F. Linton (*Journal of Botany*, 1901 and 1905), as well as his own. F. N. Hepper contributed a *Flora of Caldey Island, Pembrokeshire* (*Proceedings of the Botanical Society of the British Isles*, 1954), and Martin George *The Flowering Plants and Ferns of Dale, Pembrokeshire* (*Field Studies*, 1961). H. W. Pugsley who visited Tenby frequently in the 1920s stated that J. E. Arnett was compiling a complete Flora of the county: unfortunately it was not published. Arnett was the discoverer of the beautiful perennial centaury near Newport. Pugsley named and described the two rare rock sea lavenders, *Limonium transwallianum* and *L. paradoxum*, and discovered near Tenby a rare gentian (*Gentianella uliginosa*) which had not previously been found in the British Isles.

5

Life on the Seashore

by J. H. BARRETT

SOME of the rocks along the Pembrokeshire coast are acid, some are basic; some are hard and smooth, while others are friable, pitted and broken in texture. Two great disturbances in the earth's crust have up-ended, folded, cracked, and faulted the rock systems, leaving us with angles of dip that vary from the horizontal up to more than the vertical. Some of our rocky shores face south, some north, some west, and others east. All these variables combine together in every permutation and shade gradually from one situation to another so that Pembrokeshire has a range of kinds of rocky shore that is the envy of other counties.

Where the Bristol Channel meets St. George's Channel 35 gales on average blow every year, of which 21 come from the south-west or west. The outer coasts of Pembrokeshire are exposed to the massive attacks by storm waves that crash on to the rocks with hammer-blows of up to 25 tons to the square yard. Yet elsewhere, because the coast is so peninsulated, salt water penetrates into the heart of the county and we have long stretches of rocky shore where plants and animals that would otherwise be smashed or washed away are able to flourish beyond the reach of any storm waves.

Yet one other geographical advantage adds variety to our shores. We are so placed in the movement of oceanic currents and sea temperatures that the sea-water is warm enough for some southern creatures to survive and yet not so warm that some northern creatures cannot flourish. "The temperature of the water along any shore is the primary influence in determining the nature of the population which inhabits it."[1] Ours rises to 20°C in some summers and rarely falls below 6°C, measured at 3 feet below the surface.

The cold-water common starfish (*Asterias rubens*) and, despite its name, the warm-water spiny starfish (*Marthasterias glacialis*) are both found in Pembrokeshire. The butterfish (*Centronotus gunnellus*) is at its extreme southern limit here, the male guarding the yellow eggs which the female had attached to the underside of a stone very

[1] Stephenson, T. A.: "The world between tidemarks", in *Essays in Marine Biology* (Richard Elmhirst Memorial Lectures), ed. S. M. Marshall and A. P. Orr. Edinburgh, 1953.

low on the shore; while its relation Montagu's blenny (*Blennius montagui*) only just reaches us from the south. The Mediterranean spiny spider crab (*Maia squinado*) is unusual in the Isle of Man but in Pembrokeshire, particularly in summer, is a pest of lobster fishermen since it fills their pots, sometimes to overflowing. The common octopus (*Octopus vulgaris*) and the electric ray (*Torpedo nobiliana*) both find it only just warm enough to reach us in summer. The common oyster (*Ostrea edulis*) breeds as long as the temperature is 15–16°C or more. There used to be a large commercial fishery inside Milford Haven, but inevitable tainting by oil has made its re-establishment now impossible. The Portuguese oyster (*Gryphaea angulata*) lives here but cannot breed because of the cold.

On average the spring tides in Pembrokeshire rise and fall vertically through 20 feet, while the equinoctial springs have a range of 26 feet. At these very low levels live a variety of plants and animals that can survive only short and occasional exposure to the air; and we are lucky enough to be able to see them, since in Pembrokeshire low spring tides are always at midday or soon after (and again of course after midnight).

Between the highest level of high tide and the lowest flowering plant is a zone of the shore wetted only by bursting waves. This splash zone links the terrestrial environment above with the marine environment below. Seapinks (*Armeria maritima*), the sea fescue grass (*Festuca rubra*), the sea spurrey (*Spergularia rupicola*) or sea plantain (*Plantago maritima*), are amongst the flowering plants found lowest on the cliffs. On exposed shores they may be 50 feet above high-water mark and yet be only 2 or 3 feet above it in the most sheltered places round two or three corners from the waves. This splash zone is dominated by the lichens, composite plants in which a fungus and an alga live together to their mutual advantage. The tufted grey *Ramalina* overlaps the flowering plants as do many other species, all rather hard to determine, of encrusting greys, browns, and greens just below. Lower down again, and particularly where birds have loaded the environment with nitrogen, the foliaceous bright yellow-orange *Xanthoria* and the peppered darker *Caloplaca* dominate the level. Lower still and where wave action is more vigorous, an extensive black band of thinly encrusting *Verrucaria maura* may have black tufts of *Lichina confinis* growing with it. Other lichens flourish in the intertidal zone but are not much noted against the mass of large seaweeds or the colours and patterns of the animals. The lichens' colours are subdued; their growth is mysteriously slow. The closer an observer looks—through a hand lens better still—the more he will acknowledge their unassuming beauty.

Most of the outer shores of Pembrokeshire are too exposed to wave action for large seaweeds to survive and are instead dominated by a deep grey belt of barnacles. The warm-water *Chthamalus stellatus* is largely above the cold-water *Balanus balanoides*, both populations reacting to even short-term variations in sea temperatures and the proportion of both now being modified by the rapidly rising numbers of the four-plated Australian invader *Elminius modestus*, which was first recorded in Pembrokeshire at Neyland in 1947 and is now increasing fast enough to threaten drastic changes in the population balances of some of our shores. More than thirty thousand barnacles find attachment on a square yard of rock surface.

Below the small grey barnacles, at about low water of neap tides, the rougher, larger, brown-purple *Balanus perforatus*, which is not found in Ireland, reaches its northerly limit in Britain at St. David's Head.

Sheltering in cracks in the rocks and in amongst the barnacles of these exposed shores are many tiny winkles. The thin-shelled, dark slate-blue, southern *Littorina neritoides* may survive far up in the lichen zone. The shells of the many-coloured, larger rough winkle (*Littorina rudis*), living lower down, are strengthened against the weight of water and the battering by stones thrown by the waves by incisions between successive whorls deeper in proportion to the degree of exposure. Those two small winkles are the summer food of rock-pipits (*Anthus spinoletta*) which are themselves driven into shelter in winter, to feed on the tiny snail *Hydrobia* living in the pools on salt-marshes.

Towards the bottom of the barnacles on the exposed shores more and more small mussels (*Mytilus edulis*) are attached in clumps to the rocks, sometimes constituting an entirely dominant population, particularly where the rocks are footed at low tide by sand, and sometimes mixed with small seaweeds, particularly red ones of which none is more beautiful than *Ceramium acanthinotum*, the little tufted threads of which are barred in subtlest pink and jeweller's silver. In small pools the brown *Bifurcaria bifurcata* is almost at its northern limits. No seaweed is so unattractive or well-known locally as *Porphyra umbilicalis*, the thin slimy lank bunches of which are still gathered in St. Bride's Bay and sold on the Llanelli and Swansea markets: "a substance so papery and tender as hardly to bear the most delicate handling which is stewed and eaten under the name of laver", as Philip Henry Gosse described it in 1856. (This was the Gosse who wrote *A History of the British Sea-anemones and Corals* and was the father in his son Edmund's *Father and Son*.)

The more a shore is sheltered from the Atlantic waves, the better are the larger seaweeds able to survive. In places the rocks are entirely covered by a mattress of wracks and above all in the middle of the shore by the egg- or knotted-wrack (*Ascophyllum nodosum*), the thongs of which may be more than 6 feet long. As the tide comes in these seaweeds lift in the water's movement; any barnacle larva that was about to settle from the plankton is brushed away at the moment of metamorphosis. On shores in intermediate exposure a mosaic of seaweeds and barnacles develops. Patches of rock out of reach of the seaweeds' brushing become more extensive as increasing wave action shortens the plants, and on the unbrushed areas the barnacles thrive—the fiercer the wave action, the shorter the fronds, the more the barnacles.

Such a bare account of Pembrokeshire's rocky shores does less than justice to the marvellous variety of plants and animals that are in rock pools and amongst large stones, particularly those piled against huge boulders at very low tide mark. Many coloured patches of sponge; sea-anemones, dubiously thought by Gosse to be "glossy and plump, like some ripe pulpy fruit, tempting the eye and the mouth"; delicate, translucent oranches of hydroids; unsegmented worms that flow over the surface of upturned stones; segmented worms moving freely, some covered by scales, some with a pair of paddles on each segment for swimming, others living in tubes that vary from rock-hard calcium carbonate to mucus so soft that any disturbance destroys it; limpets, whelks, top-shells, and cowries; the unbelievable sea-slugs that digest bits of sponge and pass the silica needles that stiffened the sponge up into their own backs as their protection; brittle-stars, sea-urchins, and starfish; the sea-mats patterned as minute honeycombs and so unlike an "animal" that most non-observers do not consider the possibility of their beauty; shrimps, crabs, mysids, "sand-hoppers" (a rotten name—so few live in sand and fewer hop), and a myriad sea-slaters—all cleaning up the shore in the dark of dead and rotting waste: fish in the pools and under the stones. All these and more beside characterise the Pembrokeshire rocky shores. Gosse, writing of the Tenby shores, noted in 1856: "One can scarce examine carefully two spots on our coastline, as many miles apart, without finding some marine animals peculiar to each." That is still true today.

The pebble ridges at the base of so many bays and the sand below them are almost without life that can be seen without a microscope. In winter the gales move the stones against one another and would eliminate any animal; at the same time sand is removed into the sea so that the sandy bays so admired in summer may be 8 feet lower in winter with the underlying rock platform exposed.

But in quiet bays, notably Angle or the Gann or parts of Newport Sands or, less obviously, Lower Fishguard Harbour and the mouths of streams in Porth Clais or Solva—these places maintain a fauna as different from a rocky shore's as are the animals of moorland different from a meadow's. These animals avoid the dangers of wave action, of desiccation, and of extremes of temperature by burrowing into the ground.

Cockles (*Cardium edule*) have been gathered from of old, but their continuance is now threatened by the perpetual raking off by holidaymakers of numbers too great for natural regeneration to go on replacing. Similarly an increase in digging lugworms (*Arenicola marina*) for bait will destroy not only all the lugworms but other tube-worms too, most of all the lovely fanworms *Sabella pavonina* (Plate 12) and *Branchiomma vesiculosum* and the stonemason worms such as *Lanice conchilega* and many others.

Some of the sand-flats have dense populations of razor-shells (*Ensis*) that at the vibration of a footfall burrow down faster than their catcher can go down after them. The little *Tellinas* live there too, up to a thousand in a square yard; and the heart urchin (*Echinocardium caudatum*); the strange burrowing anemone *Peachia hastata;* the masked crab *Corystes cassivelaunus* (a splendid polysyllable to use when swearing at the cat!) that sinks below the sand and breathes by drawing water down the tube made by placing together the long antennae (Plate 13); and that very rare hemichordate *Saccoglossus ruber* which looks superficially like a worm but internally has hints of the evolution into chordates and so to vertebrates.

Particularly in years when south-west winds persist from April, the Gulf Stream and the North Atlantic Drift bring in four sailing animals that usually live in the south middle of the Atlantic. The near-jellyfish Portuguese man-o'-war (*Physalia physalia*) has a gas-filled float as sail; its relation the by-the-wind-sailor (*Velella spirans*) has a sail of stiff parchment; the blue snail *Janthina janthina* hangs below a raft of air-bubbles locked together with mucus; three or four stalked barnacles *Lepas fascicularis* depend from a single buoy.

The same combination of wind and current may strand a large brown bean *Entada scandens* that falls from bushes overhanging the sea in the West Indies and was used well within living memory of village families as a soothing bite for babies cutting teeth.

Various jellyfish are abundant in some years. In 1964 specimens of *Rhizostoma octopus*, "urging a diagonal course at the shining surface", were large enough to knock up the centreboards of dinghies racing in Fishguard Harbour.

To swim in the sea in a really dark and quiet night is to disturb countless *Noctiluca*, an animal of only one cell, a ball of jelly "not larger than a poppy seed", which, being disturbed, flashes a tiny light; the swimmer is bathed in a myriad points of light, shower upon shower of sparks like blazing diamond dust outlining his every movement. Let anybody afterwards say that the shores of Pembrokeshire are not beautiful beyond understanding. Those that have eyes to see, let them see.

6

Archaeology

by W. F. GRIMES

A. The Stone Age

THE first settlement of man in Pembrokeshire is associated with the caves in the Carboniferous Limestone outcrops of the south. The chief sites are in the Tenby region: Hoyle's Mouth (113001) and Longbury Bank in the Ritec valley, Nanna's Cave (146969) on Caldey; but there is an important outlier to the west, Priory Farm or Catshole Quarry Cave, on the Pembroke river (978019). Nanna's Cave differs from the others in being a relatively shallow recess or shelter; Hoyle's Mouth and the rest are deep sinuous water-formed penetrations of the solid rock whose human inhabitants lived usually near or at the opening, where their stone implements and food-bones are found in the soil which accumulated on the cave floor.

Amongst the species of animals represented in the deposits, many of them now extinct in Britain, reindeer and horse are the most numerous. They reflect the cold dry conditions which prevailed in the last phase of the Pleistocene Ice Age, and produced tundra and steppe vegetation which suited the herds of hoofed grazing animals that were the Palaeolithic hunters' chief source of food. The beginning of this period is placed at about 25,000 B.C. in round figures; but on present evidence Pembrokeshire man does not appear, at earliest, before about 10,000 B.C.

The implements left by the cave-people are characteristic of the cultures that equate with the final Ice Age. They include the scrapers and bone-working gravers and other forms common to the time: examples can be seen in Tenby Museum. The distinctive implement, however, is best described as a kind of pen-knife, which is well represented at Nanna's Cave and at Priory Farm Cave. It links these Pembrokeshire hunters directly with their contemporaries elsewhere in Britain as possessors of the Creswellian culture, so named from the caves at Creswell Crags in Derbyshire, where more clearly than anywhere else it could be seen that the cave-dwellers of Britain had developed differently from their contemporaries in south-western France and elsewhere on the Continent.

The accepted date for the end of the Ice Age in Britain generally is about 8000 B.C., but the change was in fact gradual. It would certainly not have been perceptible to those who lived through it. The evidence from Nanna's Cave shows quite clearly that "Creswellian" people were still about as the climatic conditions improved to a warmer and wetter version of the climate of today. A modern animal population succeeded the earlier one: bones of red deer, ox, and pig replace those of such animals as reindeer and horse in the deposits.

In archaeological terms this time of climatic improvement is that of the Mesolithic or Middle Stone Age. While caves continued in use (as they did into much later times) there was now a movement towards "open" settlement. Throughout the coastal lands of Pembrokeshire flint chipping-floors, so-called—they are probably really living-floors—are common. The flint implements, flakes, and other material found on these sites are not all of the same date, but the earliest are of the Mesolithic period, and produce the small points and other types which were intended to be mounted in bone or antler shafts to make weapons, harpoons, and the like. These sites leave no surface traces apart from the flints that are revealed when the ground is ploughed or otherwise disturbed. Their occupants lived in flimsy shelters from which they set out to hunt and fish in the low-lying land, forested and marshy in places, which for much of this time extended seaward for uncertain (and varying) distances beyond the present coast. Of the many sites known or suspected, Nab Head, St. Bride's (791111); Small Ord Point, Caldey (150966); Little Furzenip, Castlemartin (886994); and Swanlake, Manorbier (042981), are good examples. The low-lying land was the so-called submerged forest, a relic of the Ice Age which gradually disappeared beneath the sea as levels were restored with the melting of the glaciers. Submerged forests can be seen at favourable states of the surface on various beaches round the coast. Exposures of the "forest" consisting of patches of clay still carrying the remains of trees are often visible between tides at Newgale, Freshwater West, Wiseman's Bridge, and Amroth. Sometimes associated with these surfaces there are flints to show that they were frequented by Mesolithic hunters. It is likely that many of their settlements are now lost beneath the sea.

The somewhat indeterminate remains of the Mesolithic hunter/ fisher groups are succeeded in the next period by antiquities which stand in marked contrast to them in every way. These are the great stone tombs, the *cromlechau*, which were the burial monuments of the Neolithic people. The spread of knowledge of farming and its related arts from its ultimate centres of origin in the Near East was a

complicated and prolonged process which affected the British Isles
generally during the fourth millennium B.C. Many of the movements
were seaborne. For over a thousand years Pembrokeshire shared the
activity which affected all the lands round the Irish Sea, with groups
of settlers moving in the area and establishing themselves on sites
that were suited to their needs as primitive cultivators and stock-
breeders.

The tombs are more numerous in the northern part of the county
than in the south. Their chief areas of distribution are the coastal
strip and its hinterland from Fishguard to St. David's, the Nevern
valley, and the southern foothills of Presely. In the south there are
scattered examples mainly on or near the coast in Milford Haven and
between Angle and Manorbier. The tombs vary in form and it must
be remembered that what survives above ground today is normally
all that remains of a much more elaborate structure. The chamber
itself may have had other features, entrance-passages and the like,
and all were covered by mounds or cairns of stone which have been
removed in more recent times but still many years ago. The traces of
such mounds survive in many places; their full extent can sometimes
be determined by excavation and the former presence of "lost" parts
of the chambers may be revealed by the recognition beneath the
modern surface of the holes in which their stones stood.

There is room here to describe only selected examples which
illustrate the main types. At the head of the list must come Pentre
Ifan (099370) (Plate 16) as one of the most famous monuments of its
kind in the country. The chamber here consists of a capstone $16\frac{1}{2}$
feet long and weighing at least as many tons, supported at a height of
$7\frac{1}{2}$ feet above the ground by three uprights. The two supporters at the
south end of the chamber are set with a third stone between them to
form a portal. Their plan is that of the letter H, with the "bar" not
supporting and in theory therefore capable of being moved to
provide access to the chamber for successive burials. At the entrance
end also are several stones which were part of a façade defining a
semi-circular or crescentic forecourt in front of the chamber. These
features have been visible since at least the early seventeenth century.
Recent excavation has established the form of the long mound which
originally contained the chamber and the existence of various
features some of which served the purposes of ritual to do with the
dead. They include the great stone which now lies prostrate to the
east of the chamber, though this might have another explanation.
Excavation also established that the central stone of the portal could
not in fact have been moved without dismantling the whole structure.
It must be assumed therefore that, as was often the case elsewhere,

the portal is a symbolical survival and that the chamber was entered in some other way. This site in its present form seeks to give an impression of the complete character of the tomb by restoring the outline of the original mound and indicating the presence of other features in a way which leaves the restored parts readily distinguishable from the original. It is important to remember that here as in most chambered tombs the chamber itself would have been a closed structure concealed in the mound. Apart from whatever arrangements were made for access to the interior, its walls would have consisted of upright stones combined with dry walling which would have filled the spaces between them.

Inevitably the centuries-old disturbance of the site had left little behind in the way of finds. All traces of burials had vanished. A few potsherds from the chamber area combine with the form of the tomb itself to link Pentre Ifan with a much more numerous (and more elaborate) series of tombs in Ireland. These are the court-cairns, with their portal stones and crescentic façades and usually multiple chambers, and the portal dolmens, which are single chambers retaining only the portal. The problems that these monuments present are the subject of much discussion at the present time; here it can be said only that the Pembrokeshire tombs must surely be taken as evidence for colonisation from Ireland. The now ruined chamber at Garn Turne on the south side of Presely (979273) appears to be comparable with Pentre Ifan, but other long-cairned tombs also seem to be related, though they lack the distinctive portal and façade. Their chambers are normally more or less oblong or box-like, with sometimes more than one in the same mound. They have not been systematically excavated and much remains to be learned about them, but it can safely be said that they mark, taken altogether, the largest Neolithic colonisation of south-western Wales. Trellyffant (082425) is probably of the multiple-chambered class, as also is Ffynnondridian (921365); Cerrig y gof (037389) is a variant for which there are parallels both in Ireland and in Scotland. Tresewig (825284), not marked on the current maps, is an example of an apparently simple chamber which retains its portal stones.

The second great family of chambered tombs is represented by polygonal as distinct from oblong chambers which were probably incorporated in round mounds, with access provided by a passageway through the mound (hence "passage"-graves). The outstanding example is Longhouse (848335) (Plate 17), which has a large capstone supported by a number of uprights. Formerly partly buried in a field-bank, it can now be fully seen because the bank has been removed. No trace of the mound survives at Longhouse, though excavation revealed some indications of a passage; but one of the isolated monuments in Milford Haven, the Hanging Stone at Burton (972082), appears to retain a passage which owes its survival to the fact that it is incorporated in the field-bank, which protects while in part concealing it. Good examples of the apparently simple "dolmen" are Llechydrybedd (101432), Coetan Arthur (Newport) (059393), and more doubtfully Ffyst Samson (906349), all in the north coastal belt of the Park.

There is a third main class of chambered tomb, distinguished less by its form than by its association with the igneous monadnocks that dominate the landscape between St. David's Head and Goodwick. The chambers themselves are quite simple, sometimes box-like, their capstones supported on low uprights or even on natural ledges in the outcrop that shelters them. Round the megaliths there are often smaller stones which suggest the remains of a covering cairn: in their complete state they must have presented the appearance of small artificial caves. But most of them are much ruined now; and this, combined with the bracken that dominates many of the sites, makes them difficult to find in high summer. St. David's Head has another Coetan Arthur (725281) which is easily seen between low outcrops, while to the east there is a pair of small chambers high up under Carn Llidi (736279). The other most readily recognisable example is on Carn Wnda (933392). Less obvious are a series of three ruined chambers on the eastern side of Garn Wen (947390), and another on Garn Gilfach (908390). There is one isolated example of the same type amongst the small number of tombs in the south. The King's Quoit at Manorbier (059973) was supported on the ledge of a red sandstone outcrop which descends the headland obliquely towards the sea. The capstone has been drawn forward by the collapse of its outside supporters.

Other tombs besides those mentioned in this brief summary will be found on the Ordnance Survey maps, but it is certain that many more have been destroyed in the past, their former existence attested only by field-names or the statements of early observers. But while until relatively recently the tombs were the chief source of information for the Neolithic period, more is now being learned from other sources. Chief of these is Clegyr Boia (737251). The site is a small igneous monadnock which owes its name to Boia, an Irish freebooter whose stronghold it traditionally was (page 58). Before his time the area had been occupied by a small group of Neolithic people, the remains of whose simple huts were found beneath the later features. Associated with the huts were stone axes and pottery, each interesting on its own account. The material of the axes is of local origin, identical with that of a growing number of widely scattered implements. On the analogy of other places (see below) it is likely that they are the products of an axe-making industry or factory the site of which has not yet been identified, though it is likely to be somewhere at the eastern end of the Presely Hills. The pottery consists of round-bottomed bowls of a type found also in some of the chambered tombs. There are parallels for it in Ireland and in Cornwall, demonstrating that the Clegyr Boia people were probably of the same group as the tomb-builders, linked culturally with others in the countries round the Irish Sea.

Pottery similar to that from Clegyr Boia has come from some of the Caldey Island caves. From this and other evidence it would seem that, although tombs are rare in the south today, Neolithic people were fairly generally distributed over the coastal lands (including the shores of Milford Haven) as well as over the Presely foothills. The people in question would have belonged to the various western groups of colonists who no doubt amalgamated in time with the descendants of the Mesolithic population. In recent years, however, pottery of the so-called Peterborough type from caves on Caldey and at Bosherston shows that other elements, hitherto recognisable no nearer than the Vale of Glamorgan, were reaching southern Pembrokeshire from the east.

The importance of the Presely Hills belongs to this time. Two centres of axe-production were here, though the sites of the actual factories have not been located. For one the raw material was the "spotted dolerite" which has acquired fame as the most distinctive of the "foreign" stones of Stonehenge; the rock used by the other is rhyolitic tuff which is likely to have come from the eastern end of the range. The products of both are widely distributed and like other factories of their kind they exemplify another aspect of Neolithic organisation.

It is now one of the widely-accepted facts of prehistory that the igneous rock outcrops of Presely were the source of the "blue" or "foreign" stones incorporated in the circles of Stonehenge. Between them these outcrops, with Carn Menyn (144326) the largest of them, have produced almost all the different types of foreign stones at Stonehenge, more than 80 in all, weighing in the aggregate something of the order of 250 tons. The shortest practicable distance involved in this feat of transport could not have been less than 180 miles; and the geological facts having been established, the threefold question: when? how? why? at once presents itself.

The answers are not easy. As to the date, the bluestones first appear at Stonehenge in the second period of the monument, which

has now been established at about 2250 B.C., but the occurrence of a
large bluestone boulder in a long barrow at Heytesbury suggests that
bluestones were being transported to Wiltshire some hundreds of
years earlier, long barrows of this type in general being dated to the
early part of the third millennium B.C. A possible explanation of this
discrepancy is that the bluestones were used on another site before
they were brought to Stonehenge; but this site has yet to be found.

As to "how?", convenient as the Pembrokeshire rivers appear to
be, topographically speaking, as fast-flowing upland streams with
many shallows, they do not lend themselves to water-transport until
they enter the tidal estuary of Milford Haven. An overland route to
the estuary therefore seems to be indicated. The modern highroads
across Presely to the tidal limits of the Western Cleddau near
Haverfordwest, or of the Eastern Cleddau below Canaston Bridge,
modified in detail, have all the characters of early routes. They are
linked to the bluestone area by the so-called Flemings' Way, which is
certainly prehistoric in origin: the more recent grooves and holloways
that mark its course—and it can be traced much further in both
directions—still provide the most economical way of walking the
hills. The land journey involved, with the stones carried on sledges,
would not have presented serious problems for the organisers of the
bluestone exploit. That the stones were brought southwards seems
to be proved beyond question by the fact that two of the foreign
stones at Stonehenge are derived not from Presely, but from Mill
Bay, Cosheston (000050). Somewhere at the head of Milford Haven
therefore it seems likely that the sledges became rafts. For a number
of reasons the remainder of the journey would have been best
accomplished by a sea-voyage coastwise up the Bristol Channel for a
narrowed crossing to a landfall on the "English" side.

As to "why?", at one time the Presely region was thought to have
been an area of special sanctity in ancient times because it contained
so many stone circles; but in a land so strewn with small outcrops and
erratics it was inevitable that the number of such monuments would
be much exaggerated. Stone circles of the genuine variety are referred
to later: here it will suffice to say that there are no circles on the
range itself. Nevertheless, and difficult as it must always be to see
into the minds of past non-literate peoples, it seems likely that
Presely was indeed endowed by Neolithic man with a certain sanctity.
The background to this belief is the veneration that primitive people
commonly attach to natural features that appeal to their imagination
or impress them for their usefulness: it may be reflected in the
fondness shown by the tomb-builders for the rock outcrops along
the north coast. Presely as a whole dominates its countryside,

PLATE 16. Pentre Ifan cromlech

PLATE 17. Carreg Samson, Longhouse, Mathry

PLATE 18. Moel Drygarn hill-fort

PLATE 19. Bullslaughter Bay camp—a promontory fort

opposite page
Top
PLATE 20.
Walton East
rath

Left
PLATE 21.
St. Govan's
Chapel

Right
PLATE 22.
The High
Cross at
Nevern

PLATE 23.　Nevern Church

PLATE 24.　St. David's Cathedral

particularly when seen from the south, but is itself dominated in its eastern part by its carns, Carn Menyn the chief of them, which for some people even today have something of an eerie quality. The carns were exploited by Neolithic man as a source of valuable raw material for stone axes, itself invested with a kind of magic. Stones of this sort, from places so regarded, may well have seemed desirable possessions for distant communities to whom knowledge of them had come.

From Stonehenge it is natural to turn to stone circles, already briefly mentioned, and to standing stones. Of the former there is only one certain example: Gors Fawr, Mynachlog-ddu (135294). Gors Fawr is typical of the circles that occur in the upland areas of Wales. It has 16 spaced stones, mostly a good deal less than 3 feet high, with a diameter of about 70 feet. To the north-east somewhat over 440 feet away are two outlying standing stones, each over 5 feet high, which are prominent in relation to the circle and likely to belong to it. The only other circle in the area lies across the county boundary at Meini Gŵyr in Carmarthenshire (142266), an embanked circle of a type that seems to have been incorporated in a round barrow at Letterston. At Dyffryn, Henry's Moat (059284) is an example, rare for this part of Wales, of a cairn-circle, in which a ring of upright stones encloses, or is incorporated in, a round barrow. Stone circles in general are likely to be of the Bronze Age in a broad sense; cairn-circles also, with rare exceptions.

Standing stones (*meini hirion*), the last class of prehistoric stone monument, are at once very numerous and very difficult both to interpret and to date. A recent systematic list, eliminating cattle-rubbing stones and the like, gives a total of over 70 for Pembrokeshire, their distribution mainly in the north of the county with only a scatter to the south.

The stones may occur singly, in pairs, or more rarely in larger numbers in the form of stone rows or alignments. Parc y Meirw, Llanychaer (998359), is an alignment of 8 stones, the tallest almost 8 feet in height, in a line of over 140 feet. The stones, some of which have long been prostrate, are now incorporated in a road-bank and are therefore difficult to see. There are rare examples of other stone groupings, but pairs of stones are relatively frequent and must have some special significance, particularly since the stones commonly conform with a regular pattern, one being slight and tapering, while the other is more massive. They are thus reminiscent of the so-called "male" and "female" stones at Avebury. Examples are Cerrig Meibion Arthur (118310) on the floor of the Afon Wern valley; the Waun Lwyd Stones (157313), near a source of the Eastern Cleddau;

and the Upper Lodge Stones (861142) at Haroldston West, now incorporated in a road-bank.

The dates and purposes of single standing stones are no doubt various. In other regions the frequent association of standing stones with ancient tracks seems to suggest that they were set up as way-marks. Others have been found to have burials at their feet; but it is not always clear whether the stone marks the burial or the burial is in some way dedicatory and related to the function of the stone as an idol or cult object. The only Pembrokeshire stone which has been excavated, Rhos y Clegyrn, St. Nicholas (913355), produced evidence of elaborate ritual practices in the area surrounding it. The names of standing stones sometimes associate them with death and burial: Bedd Morus, Newport (038365). But such names are of course relatively modern, as are the names that attach the stones to individuals, whether mythical or historical.

Dating problems are well illustrated by the Hang Davey Stone, a small monolith now incorporated in the south bank of the Haverford-west–Broad Haven road (895146). The stone carries a small incised cross which may indicate that it is of post-Roman date, but might also mean that it is a pagan stone which has been Christianised. In any case, the name embodies a legend associated with other stones, presumed to be prehistoric, over a wide area: they include one in the Cotswolds near Northleach. According to this, "Davey" was a sheep-stealer who carried his sheep slung round his neck by its tied feet. He paused to rest against the stone and while he did so the animal struggled and slipped to the other side of it. Unable to move the heavy sheep in this position, Davey was throttled by it.

Amongst the more impressive standing stones within the Park are Bedd Morus; the Lady Stone at Dinas (996377); the Rhos y Clegyrn stone already mentioned; Maen Dewi (775274); the Harold Stone at Haroldston West (861147); the Mafesgate and other Long Stones in the St. Ishmael's–Sandy Haven area; and in the Castlemartin peninsula, the Devil's Quoit (163964) and the Harold Stone (968959), near Bosherston. The balance of probabilities is that most of the standing stones are of Neolithic or Bronze Age date, with the emphasis much on the later period. Kilpaison barrow (page 47) illustrates the relation between standing stone and round barrow which is met with in various forms elsewhere.

B. Bronze and Iron Ages

While for the Neolithic period knowledge of living sites is being acquired almost by accident to add to what can be gathered from burial monuments, for the succeeding Bronze Age burial monuments and chance finds remain the only sources of information. The "flint-chipping floors" already mentioned produce implements that are recognisably of this time, for flint did not go out of use for such things as arrowheads and scrapers in the early ages of metal. It must be assumed that settlements continued to be undefended, or at least to have nothing more than an enclosing palisade of which no surface traces survive. There are as yet no earthworks or walled enclosures which can be recognised as of the Bronze Age.

The Bronze Age antiquity which is an indicator of settlement is the round barrow (superficially at least of earth) or cairn (of stone). Such mounds in Pembrokeshire are usually simple, resembling an upturned bowl or saucer which may be as much as 80 feet across and 6 feet high. On the moorland, though mutilated, they often retain their shape; on cultivated land they have usually been softened and reduced by prolonged ploughing to the point at which in extreme cases they may be unidentifiable. Their siting is often interesting. Round barrows are commonly found in positions where they can be readily seen, either on high ground or near to ancient trackways, and there are examples of both kinds of location in Pembrokeshire. Barrows (or more usually cairns) break the skyline of the Presely Hills at various places along their length: the three largest cairns in the county occupy the top of Moel Drygarn (157336): though they lie within the confines of the Iron Age hill-fort they are probably of Bronze Age origin. The largest single group of barrows in the north, at Crugiau Cemais (125416), beside the road from Cardigan to Nevern, occupies a prominent knoll above the Nevern valley, though curiously it is not marked on the current one-inch Ordnance Survey maps. The Presely barrows have in many places a secondary relation with the Flemings' Way. In the south the barrows of the Ridgeway between Lamphey and Tenby have a similar dual relation with high ground and with an ancient road. The Ridgeway here is indeed a perfect example of its kind, but it can in fact be extended both eastwards (to Laugharne and St. Clears) and westwards (to Pembroke, Hundleton, and Angle) as a line of communication which, like the Flemings' Way, traverses the length of the county. Two large groups of barrows, at Dry Burrows (948997) and Wallaston (925003), near Hundleton, stand in close relation to the western sector of the South Pembrokeshire Ridgeway, but are not visually or topographically prominent. The Dry Burrows group, with its outliers, is the largest of its kind in Pembrokeshire. Barrows on high points are often called Beacon, Bickney, or the like. The Ridgeway has Norchard Beacon (073001) and Carew Beacon (042008), which is said to have been used for warning signals in the Napoleonic Wars. Corston Beacon (933999) is a neighbour of the Wallaston group, in the Angle peninsula. "Bigney", east of Llanrhian (831314), relates to a long-recorded barrow nearby; the name "The Beaconing", applied to a house immediately east of Steynton (921077) on the six-inch Ordnance Survey map, led to the discovery of a round barrow in the field immediately to the north of it. But not all barrows are prominently situated. The reasons for the siting of many can only be guessed at. As indicators of settled occupation they suggest that the Bronze Age population was perhaps more widely spread than that of Neolithic times, even in places reaching some of the remoter inland areas.

The date of a barrow within its period cannot be determined from its external appearance. Uncomplicated as the mounds may appear superficially, their internal structure is often elaborate, reflecting ritual practices to do with death, while the objects associated with the burials may shed light on the local culture and its relations with other areas.

In the early Bronze (or Copper) Age—metal first appeared in Britain a little after about 2000 B.C.—body-burial was the normal practice. The earliest of these burials are often especially significant because in them may be seen the various threads, old and new, that made up the pattern of Bronze Age life, not so easily to be discerned later, at least from this source.

Three sites are relevant here. At South Hill, Talbenny (831112), now destroyed, an elaborately constructed mound with a stone revetment and a circle of stake-holes enclosing it produced a burial accompanied by a pot of the type known to archaeologists as "beakers" and recognised as characteristic of a new group, the so-called Beaker people, who reached Pembrokeshire probably by way of the coastal plain from the east. A small cairn on Linney Burrows, Castlemartin (892973), is said to have contained a crouched skeleton which was accompanied by a crude bucket-shaped pot recognisably descended from the beakers. The third mound, Corston Beacon, already mentioned, covered a large stone-built grave in which were the remains of a male skeleton, curiously extended on its back, with a knife-dagger of copper or bronze of early type, still retaining part of its original handle. The form of the grave suggested that it owed something to the early chambered tombs. The three barrows together thus summarise the variety of influences that were at work at this time. Talbenny and Linney tell of new people added to the already mixed Mesolithic/Neolithic stock. All three exemplify the practice of single burial under a round barrow replacing that of collective burial which characterised the chamber tombs; but Corston shows that the new rite could be associated with a tomb whose ancestry lay in the Neolithic past and with the new metal which was being brought probably by trade. Pottery from other burials, about which less is known because they are old finds, shows that the Irish influence recognisable in the chamber tombs continued into the early metal age. A famous "food-vessel" of Irish type from one of the barrows on the Ridgeway is in Tenby Museum, and other food-vessels of Irish ancestry were found in a barrow, now destroyed, on North Hill Farm, near Templeton (096108).

At about 1500 B.C. the burial site changed—or at least cremation, which had in places been practised before, then completely replaced body-burial. The custom of putting grave-goods came, with rare exceptions, to an end. The burnt bones were often buried in a simple pit; otherwise their accompaniment is the crude pottery urn in which they were put into the ground, with sometimes a small, often highly decorated, cup which evidently served a particular ritual purpose. Earlier generations of antiquaries called these pots "incense cups"; their successors prefer the non-committal "pygmy cup".

An example of both pit- and urn-burial is provided by the Kilpaison barrow near Rhoscrowther, in the south (889007). The primary burial at the centre of the barrow was in a pit in the old ground surface beneath the mound. Associated with it, in a head-and foot-stone relation, were an upright pillar and a boulder which lay on the surface. The stones were buried in the mound and were therefore completely hidden from view, a curious arrangement which seems to suggest some survival of the idea of the standing stone as a burial marker, the confusion of two distinct practices, or even the possibility that the stone itself had some significance as a cult object. As with other barrows, the mound once constructed acquired a sancitity which attracted other burials to it. Sunk into its surface therefore were several later cremations, either in pits or in pottery urns, of middle or late Bronze Age date. The final burial was that of a skeleton enclosed in a stone-lined grave. It was of Dark Age or early Christian type, so that the mound must have held its meaning and significance as a burial place amongst the people from about 1500 B.C. to perhaps 500 or 600 A.D.

In the north a seventeenth-century account records the finding of urns in a barrow or barrows of Crugiau Cemais. An urn which has long been in the old collections of the Ashmolean Museum at Oxford has some claim to be regarded as one of these. Most of the cairns on Presely have hollows at their centres as witness to their having been disturbed in the past. Many of these activities have gone without record, but some of the "excavations" were the work of the historian and antiquary Richard Fenton, whose *Tour* contains a graphic description of the opening in 1806 of the cairn which occupies the summit of Foel Cwmcerwyn (094312). As with almost all of Fenton's finds (the exception is a small stone axe-hammer from the Bigney Barrow, Llanrhian (page 46), now in the National Museum of Wales), the urn from the burial has not survived; but a drawing shows it to have been an example of the relatively rare so-called encrusted urn, decorated with applied strips and other elaborate ornament, which is evidence for contact with Ireland continuing well into the Bronze Age.

Parallel with activity centred largely upon Ireland there were other movements of continental origin which, beginning in the late Bronze Age, continued into the Iron Age. Both trade and new peoples were involved. In the event iron replaced bronze as the dominant metal and a language probably ancestral to Celtic became the language of the country. Such changes are gradual and cannot be dated precisely, but the prehistoric Iron Age may be said to have begun by about 500–400 B.C.

In Pembrokeshire the only evidence for this first, transitional, phase, in which Bronze Age influence can still be seen to be present, comes from Caldey. A few sherds from Potter's Cave (143971) are late examples of a type of distinctive pottery of this time. For the rest, in the Iron Age the Bronze Age situation is reversed: burial sites are unknown; settlements are abundant and readily identifiable. Chief of these are many of the "camps", "promontory forts"—not military structures, but defended settlements—and "raths" of the Ordnance Survey maps, recognisable by the banks and ditches behind which were the huts of their inhabitants. The banks are now smoothed with time, but the main defences were usually stone-faced walls; and the ditches, now barely recognisable, when cleared of their accumulated silt formed wide and deep obstacles to any attack on the site. The defences in many places are quite simple, but many also are provided with systems whose aim it is to make the best use of the position and in particular to provide maximum protection for the entrance, which is usually the point of weakness in any fortification. The hut-sites are usually revealed only by excavation but are sometimes recognisable as hollows or platforms in the modern surface, or even as stone rings.

The word "rath" has been mentioned and something more should be said about it. The term is at home in Ireland, where it is applied to a distinctive type of strongly defended enclosure. It seems to occur otherwise only in Pembrokeshire, and particularly in the middle zone of the county, where it denotes ancient earthworks of all kinds and dates. Today, pronounced locally "wraith" or to rhyme with "path", it is of genuine antiquity, occurring as it does in George Owen's *Description of Penbrokshire*, written in the reign of Queen Elizabeth I, rather than a late antiquarian introduction.

Some of the raths are quite clearly of mediaeval date: the one at Walwyn's Castle (873110), for instance, or St. Leonard's, "The Rathe", so called by George Owen, near Crundale (985189), both of which are earthwork castles of the motte- or ring-and-bailey type. Actually within the Park area the raths are mostly coastal promontory forts or cliff-castles which rely in part on the natural strength of their position for their defence. They are likely to be of the prehistoric Iron Age, with some continuing in occupation into the Romano-British period. But some that from their form and position might be thought to be post-Roman (Dark Age or mediaeval) may also be early: the warning that this might be so is given by Walesland rath (912170) which was found on excavation to have been occupied in the first century B.C. and again in the second century A.D. Walesland was an oval enclosure with simple defences consisting of a single bank and ditch.

In the coastal areas of the Park, then, fortified cliff-sites are frequent, whether called rath, promontory fort, or (in the Welsh area) "castell": the names in themselves have no archaeological significance. There is a string of raths along the southern coast of St. Bride's Bay from Black Point, Haroldston West, southwards to Great Castle Head, West Dale. On the St. David's peninsula there are interesting sites at Porth-y-rhaw (787242), Penpleiddiau (763240), Castell Heinif (724247), and St. David's Head (722279). The series is continued along the north coast with a number of "Castell Cochs" and an earthwork called Caerau, near Abereiddi (777307), which in its defensive arrangements closely resembles Castell Heinif. Many sites are elaborate and each is worthy of study for the way in which (as has already been said) its builders have disposed their ramparts and ditches and organised their entrances to make full use of strengths and counter weaknesses.

The outstanding example in the north is the St. David's Head promontory fort, Clawdd-y-Milwyr, the "Warrior's Dyke". Its stone-built defences suggest two "periods" of construction: the massive innermost rampart seems to cancel out the two slighter walls outside it. In the rampart (and in the entrance) the remains of a dry-stone facing can be seen. Behind the rampart are the platforms of under a dozen round huts with the remains of their walls, forming a compact settlement on the otherwise almost barren rocky headland. To the east, a quarter of a mile away, a strong now ruined wall is drawn obliquely across the promontory. It has two huts towards its northern end, and in defining the immediate territory of the settlement perhaps also provided an enclosure for stock. Beyond that again on the slopes of the valley that opens to Porth Melgan are the ruined walls and banks of an ancient field system. It is likely to be of two periods, with the more obvious stone rows probably marking an attempt at more recent (though still quite old) enclosure. The older activity is represented by smaller fields, mostly on the south side of the valley and not easy to recognise in the vegetation, of the so-called Celtic type. These have every claim to be regarded as the fields of Clawdd-y-Milwyr. The interest of the complex as a whole lies in the picture that it presents of an Iron Age community with its related territory: one of many such whose outlying fields, away from the cliff-lands, have been swept away by centuries of later cultivation. It is incidentally worth observing that the "modern" stone-walled fields immediately to the south of the ancient fields on Carn Hen and Carn Twlc retain the irregular "early" pattern in contrast to the large straight-sided enclosures that today are characteristic of the St. David's peninsula as a whole.

The finds from the excavation of St. David's Head are in Tenby Museum. Such as they are they suggest a mixed economy in which stock-breeding played a part. For dating purposes they are indeterminate, but a period of occupation in the pre-Roman Iron Age seems most probable.

The other outstanding series of cliff-sites is on the south coast from Linney Head, Castlemartin, to Greenala Point, Stackpole. Greenala (007966) is a site of remarkable elaboration, with powerful earthworks which enclose areas that for their smallness seem quite out of proportion to the scale of the defences. Of other promontory forts elsewhere the same criticism might be made. Fishponds Camp, Bosherston (971949), is a much larger area which was apparently occupied (on the evidence of a limited excavation some years ago) during the earliest Iron Age (fourth–third centuries B.C.). Its defences are of more than one period. The position, between valleys which were once open to the sea, would have been suitable as a landing-place and base for newcomers seeking settlement sites. In its size, defences, and siting Bosherston resembles two other promontory forts: Great Castle Head, St. Ishmael's (848060), and Deer Park, Marloes (758090), which also command good landing-places for people coming by sea.

To the west of Bosherston the coastal sites are at present accessible only in limited conditions. They vary in type. Flimston Bay camp (930945) has multiple defences behind which a number of hut-hollows can be seen. To the west, Linney Head camp (888957) is a dual-period site: there a univallate promontory fort was replaced by one with double defences; the almost levelled remains of the one are visible behind the more prominent but much mutilated stone ramparts of the other. This is a succession commonly met with in Iron Age fortifications: according to it simple defences are generally early; elaborate defences are developed from them. Neither site has been excavated and both are likely to be prehistoric, but the camps at Crocksydam, on Bullslaughter Bay (935943) (Plate 19), and Buckspool (955934) warn against too facile generalisations about dates. At Crocksydam there are only a slight stone-faced rampart and ditch; a small excavation some years ago yielded pottery which showed that it was occupied in the third–fourth centuries A.D. Buckspool, also with a single rampart and ditch, but a somewhat stronger site than Crocksydam, seems to have been lived in rather earlier, in the second century. People might evidently build themselves simple defences at any time.

The promontory fort is a natural form of defence in a coastal area, but where topographical conditions similar to those of the cliffs occur inland they are often used in the same way. Where two steep-sided valleys meet to form a more or less triangular area, that too can be defended by ramparts drawn from one valley-side to the other; or bowed defences may be thrown out from the straight edge of a steep scarp, so that the plan is that of a segment of a circle, the scarp forming the chord. Common as these arrangements are to coastal and inland situations alike, there is no reason to think that the settlements they represent were any different in date or background.

The other main type of Iron Age defended settlement is the hill-fort, which may be simply defined as a fortified enclosure the defences of which are usually continuous (apart from entrance-breaks) and wherever possible rely upon hill-slopes to add to their strength. In real terms the distinction between promontory fort and hill-fort is an artificial one, for it can readily be shown that the one merges into the other; and they were the work of the same peoples.

The one typical hill-fort in Pembrokeshire is Moel Drygarn (157336) (Plate 18). It occupies the most easterly knoll of the main Presely range, the stone ramparts of its three enclosures taking full advantage of the natural strength of the position. Within the main enclosure are the three cairns mentioned earlier; the other enclosures lie down the slope to north and east. The ramparts are much ruined, but the feature of the site is its many hut-hollows and platforms, which suggest a large population, though it must be remembered that they may not all be of the same date. Finds from excavations conducted at the end of the last century, now in Tenby Museum, suggest a date in the first century B.C.

The two other large hill-forts in Pembrokeshire are Garn Fawr, Llanwnda (895388), and Carn Ingli above Newport (062372), both set on eminences of igneous rock which dominate their neighbourhoods. The former has both dry-stone walling and bank-and-ditch defences, with some suggestion that the one is later than the other. The main entrance is by way of the relatively gentle slope on the east side; elsewhere full use is made of the rocky crags, whose precipitous outward faces are linked by the walls. Carn Ingli has a single wall, well preserved in places, its plan that of a series of enclosures in which also outcrops play their part. Recognisable hut-sites are abundant both inside and beyond the defences; they are less so at Garn Fawr. But the period (or periods) of both settlements is uncertain: from analogies elsewhere it is quite possible that excavation might show that they are of post-Roman date.

Igneous monadnocks elsewhere in Pembrokeshire have been fortified, though not on the Garn Fawr/Carn Ingli scale. One such is that at Great Treffgarne Rocks (956250), above the gorge of the Western Cleddau in a region which abounds in small earthworks. It has bank-and-ditch defences with an outwork covering the entrance. Close at hand outside it are hut-circles and traces of early fields. Another site of particular interest is that at Carn Alw, on Presely (139337). There a stone-ramparted stronghold backed on to the tor has before it a zone of *chevaux-de-frise:* low, often pointed, stones set on end in the ground as obstacles to an attacking force, and to cavalry in particular. This is an exceedingly rare feature: the third of its kind in Wales, only the seventh, as far as is known, in the British Isles. Outside Britain *chevaux-de-frise* of this type have been recorded only in Spain. The idea may have come originally from Spain. More is said about this below (page 54).

Among the smaller earthworks, figuring under various names on the maps, there are some that have all the characters of a prehistoric hill-fort. They include some of the raths. Unlike the hill-forts so far described, these sites are mostly in relatively low-lying areas where their defences have been blurred by prolonged ploughing or other agricultural activity. Interpretation is therefore often difficult and this affects conclusions as to date: this point has already been made in connexion with Walesland rath (page 49).

Only selected sites can be glanced at here. Roman's Castle, near Tiers Cross (895106), illustrates well the effect of agriculture on what must originally have been a strong earthwork. The ramparts of the main enclosure are well preserved and impressive today, but their simplicity is deceptive, for additional outworks can be recognised in the form of annexes attached to their west and south sides, the defences of which are either so flattened as to be almost recognisable or incorporated in modern field-banks. Roman's Castle occupies a dominant position on the north side of Milford Haven; Castell-mawr (118378) is correspondingly placed on a knoll in the Nevern valley. The earthwork is almost circular; it has a double bank and ditch with simple opposed entrances to east and west, but its unusual feature is an internal bank and ditch bowed towards the west, which divides the interior into approximately equal halves. There are other strongly defended forts in the eastern part of the county for which an Iron Age date may be claimed: Castell Rhyd-brown (067223) on a spur of tributaries of the river Syfynwy is one; Caerau Gaer, Llanddewi Velfrey (139161), another. Part of the outworks of the latter is incorporated in the modern road-bank. It has for a close neighbour the multiple-ramparted promontory fort called Llanddewi Gaer (145160) which also has a prehistoric look. In the Castlemartin peninsula there are two miniature hill-forts, Bulliber (902966) and Merrion (940975). They are likely to be pre-Roman and so closely resemble one another in the details of their lay-out that they must be the work of the same group of people.

Two groups of forts have been kept until last for they incorporate features which link them with sites in south-western England, there dated to the middle part of the prehistoric Iron Age (second–first centuries B.C.). One group is distinguished by concentric widely spaced rings of bank and ditch; the other has enclosures or annexes attached to the main fortified area. Both groups often occupy hill-slopes rather than hill-tops. The best example of the "concentric" type is Summerton camp, Puncheston (990301); there are others at Caerau, Moylegrove (124454), and in the middle zone of the county at Castle Meherin, Ludchurch (147117). It is possible that the castle at Keeston (898196) also belongs. The Ludchurch site occupies a high point of the ridge that carries the South Pembrokeshire Ridgeway, with commanding views in every direction. Its much reduced banks are almost in contact with the upstanding defences of a small stronghold (Castle Meherin itself, reduced to anonymity on the current one-inch maps as "Earthwork") likely to be of mediaeval or Dark Age date. Scollock rath at Walton East (019242) (Plate 20) is a hill-slope fort with a main circular enclosure with an annexe which forms an outwork protecting the simple entrance. Lady's Gate rath, west of Treffgarne (922232), has a similar arrangement, though the remains are much encumbered by modern works, and it is likely that other sites now blurred by prolonged cultivation also belong to this series. Interest lies, as has been observed, in their resemblance to camps in south-western England—Scollock rath, for instance, has a close parallel at Helsbury in Cornwall—with the implication that the same or related Iron Age people may have been amongst the occupants of both the south-western peninsulas of Britain at that time. But it is possible that the matter can be taken a little further. It has already been seen that the rare *chevaux-de-frise* defence which occurs at Carn Alw has parallels in northern Spain. Hill-forts with concentric defences and annexes are found in the same area. Taken in conjunction with pottery and other finds of the same period, they hint strongly at links between south-western Europe and south-western Britain during the Iron Age.

In addition to the fortified sites there are open settlements which consist of scattered huts, often but not always accompanied by paddocks or fields. Far and away the most important of these is the Skomer series. Ancient fields here once covered the whole island: they are missing from the central area only because of cultivation in recent times. Associated with the fields are small stone-built round huts. They occur singly or in groups; but while there is a simple promontory fort on the Neck (736088) they are scattered about and are without protection. Hut-groups in compounds in the Presely area are marked on the Ordnance Survey maps; they are in general in a ruined state; but small single huts are spaced over the northern slopes near Hafod Tydfil (106336) where they are known locally as Twlce, and there are other huts in addition to the recorded examples, on Carn Ingli Common to the south-west of the hill-fort. It is certain that there are many more such sites to be discovered in the areas of marginal land which are now rough pasture. One at Eithbed, north of Maenclochog (081286), has been mistaken in the past for the remains of a stone circle. As with the camps, the dating of these open settlements is an uncertain business. On the analogy of sites elsewhere most are probably of the Romano-British period; but some may well be post-Roman. In any case they presumably reflect settled conditions which would have made elaborate defences unnecessary.

The effect of the Iron Age occupation must have been greatly to extend the areas used by earlier inhabitants. It is possible to visualise the settlements, with their beehive-shaped huts behind their ramparts or scattered through their fields; and for the first time to be aware of the fields themselves through the fortunate survival of systems like those on Skomer Island or St. David's Head. The clearings created for them were not confined to the relatively easy cliff-lands and hill country. While only a detailed study of all the factors will account for the location of each site, the attack was also made on parts of the central area, with its much more difficult conditions of soil, drainage, and vegetation.

In the absence of other evidence it has been necessary to describe the Iron Age inhabitants of Pembrokeshire in terms of their settlements. Very scanty finds give no more than a hint of the presence of newcomers, and nothing is known of the processes by which the Bronze Age natives and the Celts coalesced into one people.

C. From Romans to Normans

By the time of the Roman occupation the people dwelling in Pembrokeshire had become the *Demetae*, so named in the later second century A.D. by the geographer Ptolemy, who also identifies the other ancient name, *Octapitae*, St. David's Head. The eastern boundary of the tribe is not known, but Ptolemy records *Maridunum*, Carmarthen, as lying within it.

Carmarthen is also the most westerly known Roman fort. On present evidence the Roman military occupation took no account of Pembrokeshire, thus depriving the modern student of a fixed point of great value for chronological purposes. It is assumed that perhaps from the beginning, unlike other Welsh tribes, the Demetae accepted the Romans peaceably, rendering military posts within their midst unnecessary. Whether or not Pembrokeshire is found to have been garrisoned, the pottery from Crocksydam and Buckspool already cited (page 51), supported as it is by less precise evidence from elsewhere, shows fortified settlements of prehistoric type continuing in occupation through the Roman period—but in occupation by natives. The main contribution of the Roman occupation may therefore have been by way of the trade which left a trail of pottery (and coins) not only in the camps, but also, inevitably, in the caves.

At the same time, sites of unmistakable Roman character there undoubtedly were. The most enigmatic is the so-called "villa" about half a mile W.N.W. of the hamlet of Ford in the parish of Hayscastle (949265). The site is about 200 yards east of a small earthwork labelled for no good reason "Roman camp" on many older maps; but it is conceivable that the two may go together even so, with the earthwork housing a farmstead of the Trelissey or Cwmbrwyn type (see below). Neither camp nor villa is shown on the current one-inch map. The historian Fenton's description of chance discoveries made in 1806 seems to leave no doubt that here was a building with Roman characteristics in its construction, and sporadic finds since then appear to confirm the date. Today the area has an irregular surface, much overgrown in the summer, and the character of the buildings that undoubtedly existed is quite uncertain. On present ideas it would indeed be remarkable if a site so remote from the accepted centres of Roman life should prove to be that of a villa.

In fact the Ford building is not isolated. Another long-known site lies across the Western Cleddau about 3 miles to the east. This is Castle Flemish (007267), given by early antiquaries the spurious name *Ad Vigessimum*. It consists of an irregular rectangular enclosure of bank and ditch, straddling the road from Maenclochog and Henry's Moat to Wolf's Castle and beyond. Trial excavations in 1922 produced evidence of occupation in the late first to second century A.D. and traces of wooden buildings were also found. But the long-held view that Castle Flemish was a military outpost is no longer accepted and the site is now interpreted as that of a defended farmhouse. The parallel in more than one respect is provided by the site at Cwmbrwyn, near Llanddowror (254122). Interpretation of Cwmbrwyn as a military site has now been disregarded in favour of an earlier view of it as a fortified farmstead.

A more recent discovery is that of a circular earthwork at Trelissey, near Amroth (174079), within which was found a rectangular stone building not unlike that at Cwmbrwyn. It was occupied in the second–third centuries A.D. Again use as a fortified farmstead seems to be indicated; but the site is well placed to have served as a look-out post with extensive views southwards and across the sea—a possibility which does not apply to any of the others. While the presence of scattered farmsteads raises no serious problem in the south-eastern part of the Pembrokeshire peninsula, with Carmarthen, both a fort and a civil settlement, only a few miles away, it is difficult to believe that Castle Flemish and Ford could exist in isolation in the much less readily accessible setting of mid-Pembrokeshire. The evidence of Walesland rath has suggested that other small earthworks were occupied in the Roman period, but according to a pattern that was essentially native in character. It seems likely that other settlements of the Trelissey/Cwmbrwyn type wait to be found. They indicate a Romanised activity of some kind, and it will be important to see how they fit into the life of a region which on present evidence saw very little of the Roman army of occupation.

It was observed that Castle Flemish straddles the road from Maenclochog and Henry's Moat westwards to Wolf's Castle and beyond, its more southerly version (to Hayscastle) passing close to the Roman site at Ford. This road has been regarded as Roman in the past, primarily, it would seem, because of its relation to these positions; but its Roman date is doubtful on present evidence and it is nowadays omitted from the maps. Nevertheless, the existence of romanised establishments in the locality must raise the question of communications, though no clear-cut line presents itself. Older maps label the Ffordd Ffleming a Roman road, but it is prehistoric in origin and remained in use for horse and foot travellers down to relatively modern times.

If the Demetae were not subjected to a military occupation which extended beyond Carmarthen, the withdrawal of the Roman army in the later fourth century may not much have affected life in the Pembrokeshire peninsula. The most serious change might have been the loss of the coastal patrols of the Roman fleet which protected the inhabitants against the Irish sea-raiders. The evidence for the existence of such a fleet is indirect but seems fairly conclusive. A base for it in the west must be assumed and might be expected to be in Milford Haven; but the suggestion that it may have occupied the site of Pembroke Castle rests at present only on the finding there in the past of Roman coins of the third and fourth centuries.

The breakdown of the Roman system in the Celtic west led to two fundamental changes. There was a revival of Celtic culture, which had lain dormant under the Romans; it was centred upon the western Church and united the lands around the Irish Sea in a single cultural province. And the links with continental Europe having been severed, there was a renewal of contact with the countries of the Mediterranean and of Atlantic Europe. In effect this was a return to conditions which had obtained throughout the prehistoric ages, from the time of the great chambered tombs and even before. The fifth and sixth centuries A.D. saw the emergence of the different branches of Celtic from the ancient British language. Dyfed (derived through early Welsh from Demetia) harboured during this time people who spoke Goidelic, the Irish version of Celtic, as well as people who spoke early Welsh; and beginning with the settlement of the Deisi from County Waterford in the third and fourth centuries, Irish influence continued strong.

The archaeological evidence for these developments is limited. The Deisi themselves, important as they were for some centuries, have not been identified by any of their settlements. Knowledge of direct Mediterranean contacts comes only from sherds of imported pottery from Longbury Bank cave in the Ritec valley near Tenby. The forms represented are both fine-ware bowls and amphorae which had served as containers for wine or oil. The trade was probably never a large one, though its products are widely distributed in the west; it had faded by the seventh century A.D. if not before.

Identifiable secular sites are rare. On Gateholm (768071), an island at mid-tide off the Marloes peninsula, a settlement made up of over 100 rectangular huts set end-to-end or grouped round courtyards was occupied in the third century A.D. and in the sixth. The evidence for the first period is that of Roman pottery and a coin of Carausius (287–293), for the second a ring-headed bronze pin of Irish type; but the excavations which produced it were of limited extent and of uncertain value. It has been suggested that Gateholm might have been a monastic site in the tradition of other island communities, including Caldey (Ynys Pŷr). Its lay-out, which is difficult to see now that the surface of the island is no longer cropped by rabbits, is certainly unusual for an Iron Age settlement in this area. Another similar setting, Sheep Island, Angle (843016), carries a large number of oblong hut-hollows on the slopes of its hog-backed top, and these also are different from the more or less circular depressions that are characteristic of Iron Age huts. It has not been excavated.

The third site is Dark Age by tradition, but extensive excavation has failed to yield corroborative evidence of its period. Clegyr Boia, near St. David's, already distinguished for its Neolithic settlement (p. 40), is traditionally the stronghold of an Irish freebooter, Boia, who gave St. David some difficulty in his efforts to establish his monastery in the valley nearby. Boia's fort is built in the earlier Iron Age tradition. Its stone-faced ramparts enclose the top of the small monadnock, linking one crag with the next; its gate, looking down the slope to the west, was found to have flanking guard-recesses on its inner side. No finds datable to the sixth century were recovered; but the tradition remains and with it the circumstantial account of David's confrontation with Boia and of Boia's death.

The archaeological evidence for early Christianity in Dyfed is made up almost entirely of the inscribed and carved stones which were set up to commemorate important individuals, secular and religious, of the time. No buildings of the earlier period are known: they would have been small churches and cells which in many places have been succeeded and overlaid by mediaeval parish churches. The Church was organised on a monastic basis, with religious communities (*clas*) whose task in the fifth and sixth centuries was a missionary one: the results of their efforts in gaining acceptance for Christianity throughout the country are seen in the dedications of individual churches to the saints who were the patrons of the *clas*. The chief missionary church in Pembrokeshire (as a part of Dyfed) was St. David's (Mynwy); there were others at St. Dogmael's, Nevern, Penally, and Caldey (Ynys Pŷr), each with its own saint. (Teilo, the other great Pembrokeshire saint beside Dewi, was born at or near Penally, but the chief centres of his cult were at Llandeilo Fawr in

Carmarthenshire and (later) at Llandaff in Glamorgan.) At all these places the earliest surviving remains are the inscribed stones; most of them have several, though they may not all have been found on the site and may have been brought in from elsewhere.

Covering the whole period of the early Christian Church there are nearly 120 stones from Pembrokeshire, with the largest concentrations at all times in the north of the county and apart from the important group at Penally only a scatter in the Tenby-Castlemartin peninsula. The earliest stones, of the fifth to the seventh centuries, are usually unshaped pillars or slabs with inscriptions sometimes accompanied by simple incised crosses, though the two are not always contemporary. The inscriptions are of two types: Latin and ogam, used singly or combined. Latin inscriptions alone outnumber the others; there are relatively few stones with ogam inscriptions only. Simple as most of the inscriptions are, they shed valuable light on more than one aspect of the life of the time.

The ogam alphabet is made up of groups of lines or notches (up to five) set out across a medial line, on a stone the angle formed by the meeting of two faces. The script appears to have been invented in Ireland by the fifth century A.D. and occurs there on a large number of stones, mostly in the south; its language is Goidelic, the Irish version of Celtic, and the names of many of the persons commemorated in them are Goidelic. Ogam-inscribed stones thus mark the intrusion of Irish people into Pembrokeshire and are an important part of the evidence which demonstrates the strength of Irish influence during the post-Roman centuries. The Latin inscriptions, on the other hand, with their Latin names, titles, and formulae, are witness to the strength of the Roman tradition which was centred upon the Church but expressed itself also in other ways. Where the two languages occur on the same stone one may be said broadly to be a translation of the other: thus, one of the Nevern stones reads, in Latin, MAGLOCVNI FILI CLVTORI—(The stone) of Maglocunus, son of Clutorius; in ogam, MAGLICUNAS MAQI CLUTARI—(The stone) of Maglicunas, son of (Maqi) Clutarias.

The stock example to illustrate these varied strands is the famous Voteporix stone from Castelldwyran, which by the accident of later boundary changes is outside Pembrokeshire but still within Dyfed (144182): the stone is now in Carmarthen Museum. The Latin inscription reads MEMORIA VOTEPORIGAS PROTICTORIS. Here Voteporix is the Brythonic (Welsh) form. The ogam inscription has VOTECORIGAS only—(The stone) of VOTECORIX; and here the Goidelic 'c' replaces the Brythonic 'P'. Linguistically therefore the two forms of Celtic speech are in use on this stone side by side. The Latin inscription, set out horizontally in the Roman manner (whereas on most bilingual stones it is carved vertically in imitation of the ogam, which normally reads from the bottom upwards), contains the epithet "Protector": an echo of imperial Rome, first applied to a member of the imperial bodyguard, later as an honorific title. Its use reflects the ancient tradition and the regard in which it was held in contemporary society. Voteporix was a member of a ruling dynasty of the Demetae; he is an historical figure who was severely condemned by Gildas for his misdeeds. His memorial stone must date closely to the mid-sixth century.

There are 36 stones of the early type with simple inscriptions from Pembrokeshire, few of them as informative as the Voteporix memorial. The following are selected examples:

Brawdy (church porch): the VENDOGNUS stone (bilingual) and the BRIACUS stone (Latin only).

Bridell (churchyard): the NETTASAGRUS stone (ogam only, but with a simple ringed cross on one face).

Caldey (priory church): the stone of ? MAGLIA-DUBRACUNAS (ogam only, but with later (early ninth-century) crosses and a Latin inscription recording one CATUOCONUS added).

Clydau (church): the ETTERNUS (bilingual), SOLINUS (Latin), and DOBITUCUS (bilingual) stones. The last has a later stemmed cross which cuts in part into the inscription.

Llandeilo (churchyard): the stones of ANDAGELUS and COIMAGNUS, both sons of CAVETUS and presumably therefore brothers. The name Andagellus occurs also on a stone from Maenclochog which is now in the churchyard of Cenarth, Carmarthenshire.

Llandysilio West (church): the stones of CLUTORIX and EVOLENGGUS (both Latin only). Clutorix is said to be the son of Paulinus Marinus of Latium, the equivalent in Irish of Lettra and in Welsh of Llydaw (compare Llyn Llydaw in Snowdonia).

Nevern (church): the stones of MAGLOCUNUS and VITALIANUS EMERETOS (both bilingual). On the Vitalianus stone the Latin inscription reads horizontally.

St. Dogmael's Abbey (church): the SAGRANUS stone (bilingual).

Stackpole Elidyr (church): the CAMULORIX stone (bilingual).

Steynton (churchyard): the GENDILUS stone (bilingual, with tenth- or eleventh-century cross added, and below it a nineteenth-century inscription).

Intermediate between these early monuments and the carved crosses of the ninth to the eleventh centuries are many stones which carry incised crosses of a varying simplicity or crudity but are usually without inscriptions and are therefore not easy to date. At their simplest such crosses may be of almost any period: some may well be contemporary with the inscribed stones; others, like that on the DOBITUCUS stone at Clydau, are unmistakably later in that they cut across the inscriptions. The crosses on the Caldey stone, simple as they are, are of the ninth century from their associated inscription. At the opposite end of the scale in terms of ornament and execution are two rough pillar-stones with precisely executed ring-crosses with geometrical or interlaced ornamental fillings in the rings. These are two of a number of fine if fragmentary stones in St. David's Cathedral, some from the area of the cathedral itself, many from the neighbourhood of Penarthur Farm (748266), where they are presumably evidence for concentrated religious activity in the ninth-tenth centuries. While some stones have been removed into the churches on sites to which they may have belonged from the beginning, others are still widely distributed throughout the countryside. Some of these may be in their original positions; others have been re-used as gateposts or the like.

Finally there are the great stone crosses, of which the chief are those at Carew (beside the modern road to the east of the castle), Nevern (Plate 22), and Penally. They belong in date to the tenth-eleventh centuries. The Carew cross, a royal memorial, is dated to 1033–35 A.D., for it commemorates Maredudd ap Edwin, descendant of Hywel Dda, who after a short reign in south-west Wales was killed in the latter year. Other fragmentary crosses of quality are amongst the St. David's Cathedral series.

These high crosses and cross-slabs lack the monumental appeal of their Irish and Northumbrian counterparts, yet illustrate well the varied sources on which, however remotely, the monumental artists drew. The dominant and commonest patterns are interlacements, key- and fret-designs all ultimately of classical origin; but the most interesting are the debased vine-scrolls and interlaced animal motifs on the Penally crosses, which are unmistakably derived from the Northumbrian school, in contrast to the strong Irish influence that colours the monuments as a whole.

It has been suggested that the disturbances caused by the Viking invasions may have played some part in provoking movement between the different centres of the Christian Church at this time, drawing them together as never before. Place-names of Viking origin (Skokholm, Goultrop, Ramsey) are common in the coastal areas and owe their existence to Norse seafarers engaged, as time went on, in trading activity that linked centres in Wales with those of Ireland and with Dublin in particular. To this context Milford (= fiord) probably belongs; so, too, Haverfordwest, though here the name is less probably Norse, since the "ford" may well refer to the ancient crossing of the Western Cleddau. Yet the only archaeological evidence for all the activity attested by the records is a small lead object with a brass inset of a Norse dragon which was found in 1911–12 on the shore at Freshwater West and is now in the National Museum of Wales. It is probably a weight and dates to the tenth or eleventh century.

The visible impact of the Normans on the countryside is inevitably clearer than that of the Norsemen; but if the great castles and their builders may be said to belong to history, there are many earthwork castles which do not apparently figure in the records and have to be thought of in archaeological terms. They have their own importance for the contribution that they make to an understanding of the time. There are about 30 such sites in Pembrokeshire, many of them, especially in the central area, associated with churches and houses to form typical Norman nucleated settlements. The earthworks commonly consist of a conical flat-topped mound (which in its complete state carried a timber castle) to which was often attached a base-court or bailey; but the castle-mound was sometimes replaced by a ring-work, as at Castlemartin (915984) or Begelly (118072). Good examples of motte- (or "ring-motte") and-bailey castles survive at St. David's (Parcycastell) (745251), and The Rath or Simon's Castle, Rudbaxton (985188). Wiston Castle (023182) carries the remains of a stone keep on its motte; its bailey survives as an earthwork and apparently was never built in stone. Two castles occupy positions that may well have served for promontory forts in Iron Age times: the two-period work at Castell Nanhyfer, or Nevern Castle (082401), where a motte was planted on what may be the enlarged rampart of an Iron Age settlement, and Walwyn's Castle (873110). The motte-and-bailey earthwork at the last site has beyond its outer rampart a small oval enclosure which has an earlier look. It is a reminder that a number of earthworks of varying complexity occur in close proximity to early mediaeval settlements in such a way as to suggest that they go with the settlement and may even be pre-Norman in origin. There are other examples at which a succession can be recognised. At Picton the large mound castle (016135) in a topographically commanding position was replaced by the great stone castle on lower ground to the west. At St. Ishmael's (and perhaps also at Castlemartin) a different pattern presents itself. There the small church is set in isolation in a steep-sided valley. Nearly a mile away the castle mound with its attendant settlement occupies a position on an open site giving control over the surrounding country. The presence at the church of inscribed stones suggests that there, in a typically sheltered position, was the early Christian settlement. Though the church stayed where it was, for the Norman conquerors the choice of site was dictated by other more aggressive needs.

7

From Norman Times Onward

by FRANCIS JONES

ON the eve of the Norman invasion, the territory known to us today as Pembrokeshire formed part of the kingdom of *Deheubarth*, ruled by Rhys ap Tewdwr, descendant of the law-giver Hywel Dda. Although the earlier kingdom of Dyfed had been incorporated into Deheubarth it continued to retain its older land divisions as units of administration. In the north and north-west lay the *cantrefi* of Emlyn, Cemais, and Pebidiog; in the centre lay those of Rhos and Daugleddau; below the haven of Milford lay Penfro, a long curved promontory that stretched from the shores of Castlemartin to the woodlands of Narberth; and on the east lay the *cantref* of Gwarthaf extending eastwards to the gates of the town of Carmarthen.

It is worth noting that this arrangement was disturbed very little by the Normans, who based their feudal units on the earlier Welsh ones, and that several centuries later, when Pembrokeshire was formed into a shire on the English pattern, the earlier divisions became administrative hundreds, and indeed continue so to this day. Thus, despite superimposition by the conquerors, the older territorial divisions endured, a circumstance that gave stability to the basic population and, as we shall see, resulted in the remarkable survival of the native aristocracy and the farming families.

A rapid Norman thrust in the latter half of the eleventh century altered the whole political structure of West Wales, and the land known to us as Pembrokeshire became severed from Deheubarth, so that by the twelfth century it consisted of a conglomeration of feudal lordships forming part of those occupied lands known as the marches of Wales. This arrangement lasted until 1536, so that throughout the Middle Ages Pembrokeshire never achieved any unity, and its history is that of fragments, each under its own feudal lord who held the land of the King, often retaining many of the older Welsh customs, local officials such as the *maer* and *ragler*, and elements of Welsh administration that the Norman lords incorporated into the feudal structure. And so the "way of life" of the people—particularly in the rural areas—was not unduly disturbed. It was a change of masters rather than a change of population. Even in southern

Pembrokeshire where Anglo-Norman occupation was more pronounced, the native population was not so much displaced as absorbed, as shown by the names of Welshmen in early deeds and documents, and by Welsh place-names like Tenby, Pembroke, Pwllcrochan, Llangwm, which would not have survived had the occupation been as ruthless and as thorough as it is sometimes alleged to have been. The most significant of the changes wrought by the conquerors was the establishment of towns and boroughs, almost exclusively Anglo-Norman, and as these were more numerous in southern Pembrokeshire, their influence there was more marked than in the agricultural north. Furthermore, intermarriage between the invaders and the native population, such as Martin, Mortimer, Cantington, de Windsor, Stackpole, and Perrott, to name but a few, led to an early intermingling of the races, and so to a lessening of tension and a general stabilisation. The difference between "Little England beyond Wales" and the rest of the county is not racial but linguistic (page 72).

The Norman arrival was heralded by the advance of Roger de Montgomery (created Earl of Shrewsbury in 1071), who from Cardiganshire thrust boldly into Pembrokeshire with forces that proved sufficiently powerful to retain those areas that the rapidity of their onset had gained. These lands were conferred upon Earl Roger's younger son, Arnulph de Montgomery, who established his *caput* at Pembroke, where a fortalice, hurriedly built, was later erected into a formidable stone castle and entrusted to the care of his chief follower, Gerald de Windsor. Encouraged by this success, other Norman thrusts followed, and the land was parcelled out among the adventurous invaders. In the south the native population was partly displaced, while those who remained were absorbed by the Anglo-Norman followers who engaged in the arts of peace—farming, trading, and fishing—as well as those of war. These settlements were not established without opposition, and even after castles were erected and the settlers reinforced, they had to struggle to maintain their foothold against the Welsh under the princes of Deheubarth, and both the King and his barons often found themselves engaged in wars of reconquest. Superior military equipment and discipline of the Anglo-Normans, their reinforcement from England both by sea and by land, together with the internecine rivalries between the native princes, rendered the final outcome inevitable.

Consequently, there is no unified history of Pembrokeshire during the Middle Ages, although at some points it sometimes touched national history. It was from Pembrokeshire that the initial conquest of Ireland was carried out; it was the lordships of the county that formed a "firm base" for campaigns against the Welsh princes; and it was from Milford Haven that Henry Tudor set forth for the field of Bosworth, an adventure that changed the course of our national history. To appreciate the significance of this development it becomes necessary to review the lordships in a little more detail. These lordships did not come into being at one particular date; their boundaries often changed, and there were occasional creations of new lordships and sub-infeudation. Nevertheless the pattern of the political mosaic remained constant, namely the superimposition of the feudal structure on the older territorial divisions.

By far the most important of the lordships was that of *Pembroke*. As already indicated, it owed its early existence to Earl Roger and his son Arnulph. Originally, the territory under its direct rule included the land south of the Haven, that is the old cantref of Penfro, a name retained by the conquerors, to take the form of Pembroke. In the early part of the twelfth century, the lordship came to include the cantrefi of Rhos and Daugleddau to the north of the Haven, but further changes confined it to Penfro. Later the Earls of Pembroke extended their domination, even to include the more northerly lordship of Cemais, but this was always opposed, and the overlordship was but shadowy. Its chief stronghold, the fortress of Pembroke, was first built about 1190, and others were raised later within its boundaries—Carew, Manorbier, Tenby, and the smaller outpost of Upton. Pembroke was organised as a shire, much along the pattern already established in England, with its own jurisdiction, administered by a sheriff, coroner, and other administrative officers. It was organised as a county palatine certainly in 1138, and possibly earlier. This was the first area of the conquered lands to be so organised to the west of Severn, and forms the root of Pembrokeshire's claim to be the "premier county" in Wales. Nevertheless, it must be remembered that this county included only a part of the territory that comprises modern Pembrokeshire. The holders of this fief were earls, more important than the "barons" or "lords" of the neighbouring lands. The Earls of Pembroke were national figures and their names, Montgomery, Clare, Marshall, Valence, Hastings, and Herbert, form part of British history. It must be appreciated that none of these was ever resident in Pembroke, and few of them ever visited the county whence they derived their title and revenues. The first Earl of Pembroke was Gilbert de Clare who received the dignity in March 1138. On the death of the third earl without issue soon after 1185, his sister Isabel carried the earldom to her husband William Marshall. Six of the name of Marshall bore the title, until eventually it passed to the de Valence family who held it for two generations. From de Valence it passed to Hastings, the last of whom, John de Hastings, died as Earl of Pembroke in 1389, when the earldom reverted to the Crown. In 1414 Henry V conferred the dignity on his younger brother, Humphrey of Gloucester, who held it until 1447, and in that year it was granted to William de la Pole, Earl of Suffolk. The next earl, Jasper Tudor, was invested in 1452, but was attainted some nine years later. In 1468 it was conferred on William Herbert, whose tenure was brief, as he was beheaded in the following year. His only son, William Herbert, succeeded to the earldom, but in 1479 resigned it at the request of Edward IV who created him Earl of Huntingdon. The reason for the resignation was that the King wished to bestow the title on his son and heir apparent. Accordingly on 8 July 1479 the King conferred the Earldom of Pembroke on Edward, Prince of Wales, who held it until he succeeded to the throne as Edward V on 9 April 1483. This Earl of Pembroke is better known in history as one of the "princes in the Tower", where he was murdered about five months after his accession. He was also lord of Haverfordwest, the lordship having been conferred on him by his father.

After this the earldom slumbered awhile. In 1532 Henry VIII erected it into a marquessate which he conferred on his wife, Queen Anne Boleyn. On the execution of the marchioness four years later, the dignity reverted to the Crown. However, the title of Earl of Pembroke was revived, and on 11 October 1551 was conferred on William Herbert, with whose descendants it has remained to this day. He who succeeded in 1969 became the 17th earl of the last creation, and the 36th who has held the ancient title.

The history of the other lordships follows a similar pattern. The lords marcher bowed the knee only to the King, and in their marcherdoms they were kings themselves.

About 1100 Robert Fitz Martin, a fief-holder in Devon, established himself in the Nevern district where he appropriated the lands and fortified dwelling of a Welsh *regulus* who had been unable to withstand the onset. Rapacity and piety were twin characteristics of the Normans, and one of FitzMartin's first acts after acquiring power over an extensive part of the cantref of *Cemais* was to found the abbey of St. Dogmael's, probably in 1118. Although his troops were superior in both armament and discipline to the pastoral Welshmen, he had to take the field constantly, and in 1135 was fighting desperately to resist the sons of Cuhelyn and the princes of Deheubarth. Nevertheless he weathered the difficulties, a temporary peace was arranged, and with true Norman percipience he sought firmer

6A

assurance for the future by marrying his grandson William to Angharad, daughter of Rhys ap Gruffydd, one of Deheubarth's most illustrious princes. For some time the alliance resulted in more settled conditions, but he was to find that family relationship was not a certain basis for lasting harmony. Because of some disagreement Rhys ap Gruffydd marched against his son-in-law and in 1191 expelled him from his stronghold at Nevern. Whereupon William settled at nearby Newport, and on a knoll overlooking the sea built a strong stone castle which thenceforth became the *caput* of his barony of Cemais.

The lords of Cemais suffered from their Norman friends as much as from their Welsh relations, for the Earls of Pembroke sought, and often succeeded in establishing, overlordship over their neighbours' affairs. Accordingly, Cemais occasionally came under the suzerainty of the earls, as for instance in 1273 when Nicholas Martin acknowledged that he owed suit to the earl for his lordship of Cemais.

The Martins seem to have resided on their lands far more than most of the other lords, and after 1282 we find William Martin being ordered by the King "to dwell continuously" in the Welsh marches. On the death of the last male of the family in 1326, the barony passed to James, Lord Audley, a descendant through the female line from the builder of Newport Castle. The lordship was handed down by the Audleys until the death of Nicholas, Lord Audley, in 1391, when it fell into abeyance, and remained in that uncertain state until 1405–08, when it passed to his great-nephew John Tuchet, who held the title of Lord Audley. The baronial rights and franchises of Cemais were alienated in 1543, when John, Lord Audley, sold them to William Owen of Henllys, a local landowner enriched by practice of the law, father of Pembrokeshire's celebrated antiquary, George Owen. By that time, however, the prerogatives and regalities of the mediaeval lordship, together with all others in the marches of Wales, had been vested in the Crown, so that what William Owen in fact acquired were the rights and status of an ordinary lord of the manor.

The neighbouring lordship of *Cilgerran* on the banks of the Teifi in north-east Pembrokeshire had been carved out of parts of the old cantref of Emlyn, founded probably by the Montgomerys or the Clares, and was under the domination of the Earls of Pembroke. During the first half of the thirteenth century the Cantilupes were the lords, from whom Cilgerran passed to the Hastings family which held it in 1277. In the fifteenth century it became part of the possessions of the Crown. The *caput* of the lordship, the castle of Cilgerran, stood on a steep bluff overlooking a narrow gorge through which runs the river Teifi.

The lordship of *Haverford* owed its origin to the Norman invaders, and the powerful castle that dominated the tidal Cleddau at this spot is believed to have been built in the twelfth century by Gilbert de Clare, father of the first Earl of Pembroke. Like other Pembrokeshire lordships it was from time to time held as part of the earldom, and occasionally by the Crown. In 1317 Edward II specifically granted Haverford to Aylmer de Valence, Earl of Pembroke. It often changed hands, and was held at different times by de Braose, de Bohun, Hastings, and Mortimer. It was held by the Prince of Wales (son of Edward IV), who as "Edward, Prince of Wales, and Lord of Haverford" granted a charter conferring important liberties on the burgesses and enacting that the town should be incorporated.

The smaller lordship of *Narberth* was never so important as the others, although its castle occupied a strategic position in eastern Pembrokeshire. It was held at various times by the families of Mortimer and Devereux, and in 1477 by the Prince of Wales.

The lordships of *Dewsland* (Pebidiog) and *Llawhaden* differed from the others inasmuch as they were episcopal fiefs whose overlord was the Bishop of St. David's for the time being. The ancient cantref of Pebidiog had been granted by the Welsh princes to the see of St. David's, a circumstance that had an important effect on the lives of those who dwelt within its confines. It is the only part of Wales that has never been conquered by either the English or the Normans. Its inhabitants are the oldest free folk in Britain. The Normans, pious if nothing else, respected the property of the Church, so that Dewsland was spared the battles and sieges that accompanied the annexation of other parts of Pembrokeshire. No stone fortress was built on its soil; no alien garrison stood ward and watch over its inhabitants. The fact that it was the land of Dewi, the patron saint, proved sufficient to preserve it from the grasping hands of ambitious invaders. To its *caput*, the cathedral church of St. David's, came thousands of pilgrims throughout the Middle Ages when two such pilgrimages were held to be equal to one to the Eternal City. From the bay of Goodwick to the strand of Newgale, from the grey crags of Pencaer to the bold cliffs of Penmaen Dewi, an agricultural folk passed tranquil days, for here the Cross was ever mightier than the sword. While all the Norman castles are in ruins, the cathedral of St. David's remains an enduring monument to the arts of peace (Plate 24). It is true that the once magnificent episcopal palace on the banks of Alun is now nothing more than a picturesque relic, but that change was encompassed by the vicissitudes of administration rather than the battering ram and siege gun.

The smaller lordship of Llawhaden also belonged to the see, and its castle was built as a fortified residence for the bishops in the penultimate decade of the thirteenth century. The bishops had two other residences, neither being fortified, namely Trefin in Dewsland, and Lamphey "below the water" in Castlemartin.

Such was the political complexion of Pembrokeshire throughout the Middle Ages—a mosaic of lordships, each under its own lord with its own laws and customs. Thus the mediaeval history of the county is a history of fragments; there was no cohesion, no central control. It was a western "Balkans". Accordingly, no history of Pembrokeshire as such can be attempted for this period; we can only glance at certain facets of life, the main ingredient of which was a sturdy individualism.

Another Norman feature, the relics of which are still with us, was the building of religious houses. Among these were St. Dogmael's Abbey and Pill Priory (Reformed Benedictines), Haverfordwest Priory (Augustinian Canons), Haverfordwest Friary (Black Friars), Monkton Priory (Benedictines), Caldey Priory, Llawhaden Hospital, and Whitewell Hospital at St. David's. All of these owed their origin to the Normans, such as William Martin who founded Caldey and St. Dogmael's; Robert FitzTankard, founder of Haverfordwest Priory; Arnulph of Montgomery, founder of Monkton Priory; Adam de Rupe (Roch), founder of Pill Priory. In addition there were numerous subordinate chapels and chantries, dating from the age of Celtic saints, built in characteristic Welsh form, and often endowed and enriched by the Norman settlers. Among these we find the chapel at the holy well of Cwmwdig, St. Justinian's Chapel, St. Mary's College at St. David's, St. Non's Chapel, and many more. Prominent among them and enjoying considerable wealth and power, due largely to its adventurous and international character as well as humanitarian ministrations, was the Commandery of the Knights of St. John at Slebech above the waters of Cleddau. Together with the parish priests, the good monks were the main, indeed the only, civilising agents of that barbarous age, giving succour to the needy, aid to the sickly and infirm, welcoming to their cloisters the wandering bards and the illuminators of manuscripts, training and encouraging the voices of young and old to give praise to the Heavenly Master to serve whom was their mission in life.

Two features taken together help to form the larger picture, although they developed independently and largely in isolation. The first was the establishment and development of towns, the second was the basic industry of the county, agriculture. Trade and industry in addition to sustaining the wants of society also provide a sense of unity and common purpose, often helping to allay racial animosities.

A "Welsh black" among the pastures of Daugleddau and a pony on the slopes of Presely have no nationality.

The Welsh had never been dwellers in towns. Before the Norman arrival there had been no towns in Pembrokeshire, only a few villages of no consequence. The formation of towns was an alien activity introduced into the county by the Normans. Apart from siting castles in places that gave them natural protection, the Normans were also careful to site them so that their garrisons had access to the sea and could be supported by seaborne reinforcements. This meant that they were often at places equally suitable for seaborne trade, with the result that during the Middle Ages many developed into flourishing trading towns, such as Pembroke, Tenby, Haverfordwest, and Newport. The Norman retainers built their habitations around the walls of the castles to which they could retire in troublous times, and the Norman lords protected their followers by granting privileges and liberties to them. Charters were granted, sometimes by the local lord, sometimes by the King, and invariably confirmed, sometimes extended, by successive monarchs. The towns themselves were protected by strong walls and gateways, excellent examples of which can still be seen at Tenby.

Pembroke can justly claim to be the first county town in Wales, being *caput* of the first county organised to the west of Severn. It received its earliest charter in the reign of Henry I (1100–35) and the first earl incorporated the inhabitants of the town which he surrounded with an embattled wall defended by several bastions and entered by well-guarded gateways. The town flourished and, although it often suffered from warlike incursions, its castle never fell into the hands of an attacker. Within the castle walls Henry VII was born, the last of the three Kings of England to have been born on Welsh soil.

Haverfordwest, on the banks of the tidal Cleddau, received its first charter from Henry II (1154–89) who confirmed the liberties of the townsfolk as they had been in the time of Henry I; so the town was built for certain early in the twelfth century and possibly had received an earlier charter. Subsequent charters were granted to Haverfordwest by two Earls of Pembroke and by fifteen monarchs, the last being from the hands of William and Mary. Governed by a mayor, who also bore the title of Admiral of the Port, and a corporation, it became the most important trading centre in Pembrokeshire. The right to have a sheriff and two bailiffs was granted in 1479 by the Prince of Wales who then held the dignity of lord of Haverford. In 1545 Henry VIII granted a statute erecting it into a town and county of itself, which later enjoyed its own assizes, courts of Great Sessions, with a Lord Lieutenant and Custos Rotulorum.

Its prosperity and geographical position made Haverfordwest an ideal county town after the Act of Union which organised Pembrokeshire as a shire.

Other towns such as Newport, whose earlier charter was confirmed by Nicholas Martin about 1240, and Tenby, whose inhabitants were incorporated by William de Valence with the consent of his wife in whose right he had succeeded to the palatinate, developed along similar lines, while lesser castle-towns like Narberth and Cilgerran became thriving centres for local trade.

The racial composition of Pembrokeshire was greatly affected by mediaeval events. In the train of the Norman lords came Englishmen, later to be reinforced, particularly in the southern half of the county, by families from Somerset, Devon, and Cornwall, counties which always enjoyed a brisk coastal trade with South Wales. In the eleventh century, mainly in the Roose and Haverfordwest area, a number of Flemings settled, described by Giraldus as "a people, brave and robust, ever most hostile to the Welsh . . . well versed in commerce and woollen manufactories". They were too few in numbers to maintain a separate identity for long and became absorbed into the general population. It is ironical that the only family with a proven descent in the male line from a Fleming lives in the Welsh part of Pembrokeshire. In time these elements, to which was added later an Irish infusion, became welded into what the poet Drayton calls "those men of Pembroke of the mixèd breed".

The northern part of the county retained its Welsh speech throughout the centuries, whereas the southern part is entirely English-speaking. The "line" dividing these linguistic communities stretches roughly from Roch on the west to Narberth on the east. George Owen, the historian, has discussed this division in some detail, and sometimes used the old legal term land-scar (that is, boundary) to express himself. Unfortunately some modern writers have interpreted this as a proper name and have tried to impose the name "landsker" or "landscar" on this dividing line.

In fact the difference between northern and southern Pembrokeshire is not racial but linguistic. In the north we still find Welsh-speaking families bearing Norman names of Martell, Miles, Mortimer, Devereux, and Reynish; or English names of Picton, Sayce, Selby, Mabe, and Battin; while in the south monoglot English families answer to the names Griffith, Howell, Craddock, Bowen, and Rees. Thus does genealogy confound racial and nationalistic unrealities, and in Pembrokeshire the language of a man is no indication of his ancestral origin. One whose ancestors were harried by Normans now keeps a shop in the shadow of Pembroke Castle, while another, whose ancestors lorded it over mediaeval Haverford-west, herds his sheep on the uplands of Freni Fawr.

Throughout the Middle Ages the people of Pembrokeshire pursued a reasonably settled life. It is true that until the final eclipse of the Welsh princes in 1282 the land was often harried by war-bands, but there was no reconquest and the castles and lordships remained in the hands of the *advenae*. Its geographical position at the extreme south-west meant that it was far removed from those parts of Wales where the political conflicts were decided in field and court. Even during the rising of Owain Glyndwr, whose armies thrust into the very heart of the west, Pembrokeshire was never as completely in his grasp as the rest of Wales. Glyndwr had good Norman blood in his veins, for he was descended from the family of de Vale who held lands in the lordship of Haverfordwest and himself inherited the manor of Treffgarne in right of that descent. The county also suffered from the ravages of the Wars of the Roses, but the people were content to leave the issues of state to their lords whose main concern was the retention of the castles. Some of them, like Harry Dwnn of Picton Castle, took the field on the Yorkist side, which led to his death at the battle of Banbury in 1469. Another Pembrokeshire Yorkist was more fortunate. This was Jenkyn Lloyd of Blaiddbwll in Llanfyrnach, a descendant of early chieftains, who bore as his coat-of-arms a golden lion rampant between eight golden roses on a blue shield. To demonstrate his loyalty to the House of York, he changed the colour of the roses to white. So long as the Yorkists were in the ascendant he did well and was rewarded with some local appoint-ments. But after the Lancastrian triumph in 1485 we hear no more of Jenkyn and his white roses—an example of the hazards of displaying one's politics in heraldic form.

During the Middle Ages, Pembrokeshire produced two of Wales's greatest literary men. The first in point of time was Gerald de Barri, better known as Giraldus Cambrensis or Gerald of Wales. Born at Manorbier about 1146, he was the youngest son of William de Barri and Angharad, daughter of Gerald de Windsor by Nest, daughter of the prince Rhys ap Tewdwr. He became an eminent cleric and wrote numerous books still regarded as valuable sources of historical information, perhaps the best known being *Itinerarium Kambriae*. He died in 1223. The other *littérateur* was Wales's greatest mediaeval poet, Dafydd ap Gwilym, who flourished in the period 1340–70. Dafydd came of a Pembrokeshire family that sprang from ancient princes who had come to terms with the Normans and whose descendants became "King's men" and held royal appointments in West Wales. His great-great-grandfather had been Constable of

Cemais in 1241, and a decade later held the appointment of King's Bailiff.

The accession of Pembroke-born Henry Tudor, Earl of Richmond, as King Henry VII in 1485 was the beginning of a long period of peace for a country that had been cruelly racked by internal dissensions for nearly a century. The political structure of Wales—principality, Crown lands, marcherdoms—and the fragmentary character of its local government remained unchanged, seemingly unchanging. But winds of change were blowing over the land and during the reign of the next monarch rose to a veritable hurricane.

There were several reasons for the impending changes. The economic position of Britain had become stronger and her overseas trading interests added daily to her growing wealth. The Renaissance had inspired new ideas, but more important still was the attitude of the Crown towards its responsibilities. The Tudors quickly realised that the only way to eliminate civil disorders was to centralise government and control directly under the Crown, and to deprive the feudal nobility of the power to muster troops and to wage war under their own banners. With the service of able administrators and an efficient bureaucracy, the trend was towards centralisation of authority, thus increasing the power of the Crown. The Statute of Livery and Maintenance was passed to prohibit the great lords assembling and maintaining armed retainers, so a possible threat to central government from private wars was reduced. A new spirit of English nationalism was becoming evident, typified in the person of the able, ambitious, energetic Henry VIII. He was the herald of the modern age—a John Bull in Tudor bonnet.

Britain was pulled, squalling and struggling, from its outworn mediaeval background and brought into a world that demanded new men and new measures. Between 1530 and 1540 a revolution took place in Britain that was to determine its future position in the European structure. Its main architect was Henry VIII, the greatest crowned revolutionary in British history, certainly its most successful.

The first step was the complete severance of the native Church from the dominance of Rome. The substitution of the monarch for the Pope as head of the Church was an act of supreme significance, and the ruthlessness with which the policy was carried out bore ample witness to the determination of the reforming King and his ministers. The dissolution of the monasteries followed. Although most religious houses were in need of reform, there can be no doubt that their suppression was a violent measure, and, some might consider, went beyond the demands of reasonable correction. In Pembrokeshire the abbeys of St. Dogmael's, Haverfordwest, and

PLATE 25. Coracle racing at Cilgerran

PLATE 26. Invader's-eye-view inside
a tower at Cilgerran Castle

PLATE 27. Pembroke Castle

PLATE 28. Carew Castle

PLATE 29.
Tudor Merchant's House at Tenby

PLATE 30.   Blackpool mill

PLATE 31.
Porthgain Harbour

PLATE 32. Lime kilns at Solva

PLATE 33. Casting she[d] in which "pig-iron" wa[s] produced at Stepasid[e] ironworks

PLATE 34. Oil tanke[r] passing St Ann's Hea[d]

Monkton, the College of St. Mary at St. David's, and the chantries were emptied of their venerable tenants, of their treasures, lands, and revenues, while the outward expression of religious exercises, pilgrimages to holy wells and altars of saints, adoration of relics and veneration of images, were declared idolatrous practices, not to be tolerated by a monarch who, ironically, had once been declared "Defender of the Faith" by a former occupant of the throne of St. Peter. The people were stunned, but generally acquiesced in the new order which afforded them little opportunity for defying the dictates of their masterful ruler. When, over a decade later, Queen Mary attempted a counter-reformation, it found strong opposition from those who had accepted the new Protestantism, and William Nichol of Haverfordwest preferred to suffer at the stake rather than renounce his convictions.

But the measure that affected Pembrokeshire most was the so-called Act of Union of 1536, and the supplemental act passed four years later. This was the moment in history when Pembrokeshire as we know it was born. Here again, the ruthless axe fell with devastating effect. The distinction between Crown lands and lord marcherdoms, with their separate jurisdictions, was swept away and the whole county came under the rule of English law. While many feudal incidences remained in that some of the older divisions survived as manors—Cemais and Dewsland, for example—this had only a minor significance, for their incumbents could no longer raise troops, levy taxes, or execute felons. They had been "cut down to size". The King was supreme over all.

Inevitably, boundaries were rearranged. The eastern half of the lordship of Emlyn and nearly all of the fertile cantref of Gwarthaf were torn from mediaeval Dyfed and incorporated into the new shire of Carmarthen. Then, indeed as now, angry growls were heard on the slopes of Presely and the banks of Cleddau, in the council chambers of Haverfordwest and Tenby and the court leet at Newport, but these in no way lessened the determination of the monarch and his ministers to implement the new policy. Pembrokeshire came into being, its traditional cantrefi and lordships transformed into seven administrative hundreds: in the north, Cilgerran, Cemais, and Dewsland; in mid-county, Roose, Dungleddy, and Narberth; and "below the water", the long curving horn of Pembroke, which gave its name to the new political structure. By further arrangements made in 1542, Haverfordwest was formed into a county of its own (as well as remaining the "county town" of the whole shire), while Laugharne and Llanstephan (initially included in the new Pembrokeshire) were transferred to Carmarthenshire. This settlement, which rearranged the rump of the old Dyfed, has remained substantially unchanged to the present day.

As we have seen, by an accident of history, Pembrokeshire had become divided into Welsh- and English-speaking areas. Under the new dispensation the division remained as clear as ever, and indeed has never been eliminated. Yet there is not, and never has been, any line of demarcation. A southern Pembrokeshire man has as much loyalty and affection for the Prince of Wales as his northern neighbour, and the burghers of Haverfordwest will cheer the Welsh Rugby XV as ecstatically as the ploughmen of Llandeloy.

Henry VIII had close family associations with the county. Among his ancestors were the Welsh princes of Dyfed, the later lords of Treffgarne, and the Norman family of de Vale. His grandfather had been buried near the high altar in St. David's Cathedral. His father had been born in Pembroke Castle in 1457, had found refuge among Pembrokeshire folk when Yorkist rulers were baying at his heels, and it was to Milford Haven that he returned in 1485, and from there, with an army swollen by Pembrokeshire supporters, marched to decisive victory at Bosworth. Henry VIII was the first to fortify the Haven whose waters had borne his father to the sceptre and the orb.

The new organisation allowed Pembrokeshire people to participate more intimately in the governing of their local affairs. For the first time the people were able to elect Members of Parliament, to provide High Sheriffs and Justices of the Peace from among their own kith and kin. They had access to the King's courts at Westminster and to his assizes and Great Sessions held on their doorstep. Numerous lesser officials, coroners, clerks of the courts, customs officers, commissioners, captains of array, were selected from the men on the spot. It was a form of "Home Rule".

Mention must also be made, in passing, of an important event in the reign of Elizabeth I, since it had a profound effect on the northern half of the county. This was the translation of the Bible into Welsh, which more than any other single factor contributed to the preservation of that ancient language.

As a maritime county, Pembrokeshire had a twofold interest—seaborne trade and agricultural production. Throughout Tudor (and later) times, agriculture continued to be the basic industry, and with its ancillaries constituted the backbone of local economy. Production, particularly of grain, was greater than has been supposed, and the surplus, in addition to supplying the local markets, was exported by sea to other parts of Britain. The charter towns with access to the sea had enjoyed a flourishing existence throughout the Middle Ages, and now, with the general rise in national prosperity, became ports in their own right. The title of Admiral of the Port, still borne by the Mayor of Haverfordwest, bears testimony to the maritime activities of that town. Ships came to the ports of Pembroke and Tenby, and to Haverfordwest on the tidal Cleddau, laden with merchandise, homely commodities and necessities, and more exotic items like spices and wines, and bore away cattle, grain, wool, pelts, and manufactured goods.

Ships built in Pembrokeshire yards, owned and manned by local men, traded as far afield as the Baltic and Mediterranean. Such voyaging could sometimes be hazardous, as William Scourfield of Moat discovered during Elizabeth's reign. During a voyage to the then little-known coast of Barbary he fell into the hands of Arab corsairs and spent many years as a slave of those dusky infidels. Eventually he managed to gain his freedom by arranging for a ransom. On arriving in Pembrokeshire he found that his wife, deeming herself a widow, for no news had been received of her captive husband, had succumbed to the suit of the engaging Morgan Philipps of Picton Castle and married him. Morgan was loth to part with her (she was a considerable heiress in her own right) and the aggrieved Scourfield had to go to law to secure the return of his spouse.

The woollen trade had been particularly flourishing during the Middle Ages, and several families, such as the Laugharnes and Voyles, had profited so well from participation in this trade that they were able to purchase large estates and so enter the ranks of the landed gentry. By late Tudor times the woollen trade had passed its peak, and coal mining, tanning, and other ancillaries were providing opportunities for energetic and ambitious men. Thomas Cannon of Haverfordwest was another who participated successfully in trade, which led to a seat in Parliament and the joys of a knighthood, in addition to the acquisition of an extensive landed estate. Coal mining was carried on, mostly as the result of capital invested by the gentry, in the areas of Brawdy, Roch, and particularly in the south of the county, but it was not for another century that developments in mechanical techniques enabled the industry to become a significant factor in the life of West Wales.

The Tudor period witnessed an influx of newcomers to the county. Some profited by the dissolution of the religious houses whose lands were sold or leased to laymen. Among these were the Barlows of Slebech. Others arrived as officials, such as the Stepneys of Prendergast who intermarried with heiresses of Welsh families, so that their descendants became leading magnates in West Wales. Two other distinguished arrivals were Dr. Thomas Phaer of Forest Cilgerran, physician to Queen Mary Tudor, and translator of Virgil's *Aeneid* into English; and Robert Recorde of Tenby, the inventor of some mathematical signs still in use.

Pembrokeshire also proved a happy hunting ground for hordes of Irishmen, some looking for employment and others displaced by disturbances in Erin's isle. But they failed to find a place in the affections of the natives, as George Owen, a contemporary observer, tells us. Families with roots deep in mediaeval times continued to hold vast estates, and indeed to increase them, and it was they who effectively dominated all aspects of local government—the influential and able houses of Wogan of Wiston, Owen of Orielton, Philipps of Picton Castle, Bowen of Llwyngwair and Trefloyne, Warren of Trewern, Lloyd of Cilciffeth, Perrott of Haroldston, the Laugharnes, Adams of Paterchurch, Butler of Coedcanlas, Catharne of Prendergast, and many more.

No account of Elizabethan Pembrokeshire can be complete without mention of George Owen of Henllys (1552–1613) and recourse to his unique and invaluable *Description* of the county. Owen was a conceited, learned, litigious, biased, and wholly delightful individual. His father, a successful lawyer, had bought the manorial jurisdictions of the lordship of Cemais and set himself up as a magnate in the Newport-Nevern area. The gifted son, George, who walked with a limp, inherited the fruits of his father's speculation, and, dominated by a *folie de grandeur*, spent most of his time advancing the claims of his lordship to primacy in Pembrokeshire. An outstanding antiquary, he was interested in all aspects of history, present and past, and amassed a huge corpus of manuscript material which he arranged as a *Description of Penbrokshire*. This veritable treasure-house is full of curious lore and vivid pen-pictures of life. His exciting commentary on the game of *cnapan*—a barbaric form of football played between parishes—is something which the most expert modern commentators can hardly rival. Little of consequence escaped his inquisitive attention, his buccaneering pen probed into the most unlikely corners, his industry and energy were prodigious, and his work remains not only a landmark but a basis for any historical enquiry into the bygones of Pembrokeshire. He considered its people to be the salt of the earth, and himself the prime representative of those whose virtues he extolled and whose achievements he chronicled.

The seventeenth century witnessed the consolidation of the efforts of the previous century. The growing prosperity that marked the Tudor period did not end with Elizabeth's death in 1603. The county continued to flourish under the Stuarts and, despite the dislocations caused by the Civil Wars, emerged without appreciable damage to its economy. It is interesting to note that the Welsh parts of Pembrokeshire were, with few exceptions, strongly Royalist, whereas the anglicised parts produced enthusiastic Roundheads. Southern Pembrokeshire kept the flame of opposition alive when all other parts of the county lay in the King's hands. Pembroke Castle was the only fortress that did not capitulate to the royal forces, and the waters of the Haven enabled Parliamentary vessels to relieve the beleaguered garrison and to support land operations on behalf of Cromwell. Foremost among the Roundhead leaders stood Major-General Rowland Laugharne of St. Bride's, one of the ablest tacticians thrown up during the unhappy conflict.

Constancy was not a lasting quality in those tumultuous days, and men changed their political allegiances as nonchalantly as their shirts. When the second Civil War broke out in 1648, Rowland Laugharne, Colonel Powell, and Mayor Poyer (a respectable tradesman of Pembroke) abandoned their earlier partisanship, declared for the King, and garrisoned Pembroke Castle, the key to military success in the west. The importance of such a move may be gauged by the fact that Cromwell deemed it necessary to lead an expedition into Pembrokeshire. The castle's defenders soon felt the presence of his military genius, and Laugharne capitulated after a short siege. The conqueror decreed that one of the three leaders must forfeit his life, the decision to be made by lot. Laugharne, Powell, and Poyer nervously drew the papers from a Parliamentarian casque. The hapless Poyer drew the blank, and he fell before a firing squad in Covent Garden. Thereafter his descendants bore the motto, "Destiny is against me", in memory of the melancholy fate of their ancestor.

Lucy Walter, one of Pembrokeshire's most permissive daughters, attracted the notice of the Prince of Wales (later King Charles II), and consequently became the mother of the Duke of Monmouth. Her father, William Walter of Haverfordwest and Roch, who had married a cousin of the Royalist Earl of Carbery, came from a line of wealthy burgesses in the county town.

As a result of the rising of 1648, Cromwell ordered the destruction of certain castles in Pembrokeshire, so that they could never again become a challenge to the new regime. Several of them suffered in varying degree as a result of this rigorous mandate, but their formidable ramparts defied total demolition, a tribute to the work of the mediaeval masons who had erected them.

Although several local magnates suffered through fines and confiscations, the Civil Wars did not disturb the balance of the ruling families unduly, and at the Restoration in 1660 they were still firmly in the saddle. The agricultural interest, that abiding basis of Welsh life, had not been dislocated, and the towns of Haverfordwest, Pembroke, Tenby, and to a lesser degree Narberth and Newport continued to flourish as centres of trade and commerce.

One notable feature of the latter half of this century was the rise of religious dissent. Although the Nonconformists were not particularly numerous and extended their influence but slowly, they were to become a vital religious and political force in the nineteenth century.

The eighteenth century was tranquil so far as Pembrokeshire was concerned, a period of steady economic progress. Landowners consolidated and improved their properties, farmers benefited from the general prosperity and improved marketing. The towns continued to flourish and the ports were playing an even more leading role in the economy. Landing stages, quays, kilns, and storehouses were built at remote creeks like Abercastell, Solva, Porthgain, Fishguard, and Stackpole Quay. The sea was one of Pembrokeshire's great highways and, at the ports and creeks, vessels discharged cargoes of coal, limestone, and other goods, and took away grain and other produce to markets further afield. Many landowners and farmers held shares in the small craft which plied their trade along the coast of Wales and beyond. Pembrokeshire accents were heard on the quaysides of Liverpool, Dublin, Bristol, and London. Two light-houses were built to guide mariners: St. Ann's constructed mainly through the exertions of the Allen family, and the Smalls, created in 1773.

This seagoing trade continued to grow during the succeeding centuries and was displaced only after road and rail communications became so developed that the competition proved ruinous to the small shipowners. The writer's family has been intimately connected with the coastal trade. One of his ancestors in the eighteenth century was engaged in carrying cargoes of grain (to which he added the illicit, but eminently profitable, smuggling of salt); another found a watery grave at Cefn Sidan Sands during a great storm; and a kinsman owned and captained one of the very last vessels to trade in Pembrokeshire ports, the *Ben Rein*, whose peaceful operations ceased not long before the outbreak of the second World War.

The same century produced valiant sea-dogs whose names continue to adorn our naval annals: Admiral Thomas Tucker of Sealyham (who slew the notorious pirate "Bluebeard"), Admiral Vaughan of Trecwn, Admiral Sir Erasmus Gower of Glandovan, and Admiral Sir Thomas Foley of Ridgeway (friend of Nelson).

Neither must we overlook that other, though less respectable, sea-dog, Bartholomew Roberts of Casnewydd Bach, "Barti Ddu", swashbuckling buccaneer, terror of the Spanish Main.

But man does not live by bread alone. The eighteenth century saw the first concerted move to improve the educational lot of the people. Not that the county had been without schools. There had been a school at St. David's Cathedral in the Middle Ages, and another was established there before 1563 and continued to flourish into the nineteenth century. A grammar school had been founded in Haverfordwest by Thomas Lloyd of Cilciffeth in 1613 and another by Mary Tasker in 1684; Sir Hugh Owen of Orielton had founded a similar school at Pembroke in 1690. The wealthier families sent their sons to grammar schools at Cardigan, Carmarthen, Swansea, and Bristol, and later to the public schools in England.

Few facilities had existed for the poor, but now philanthropic, public-spirited people like Sir John Philipps of Picton Castle, the devout Griffith Jones, vicar of Llanddowror, Madam Bevan of Laugharne, and the Bowens of Llwyngwair took a prominent part in establishing circulating charity schools with the object of imparting elementary education to the lowly, both children and adults. These schools were held in various places—in farmhouses, cottages, barns, churches, and other buildings, mainly in the villages and country districts. Between 1699 and 1736 no fewer than 28 schools of all kinds existed in the county. Neither must we forget the laudable efforts of the Rev. John Griffith of Fagwyrgoch in northern Pembrokeshire (1732–1825), a poor curate passing rich on £42 a year, who established in 1761 a lending library of over one thousand volumes purchased from his own slender resources, and gave private tuition to the children of cottagers and farmers.

Both the Church and the Nonconformists (now a strongly organised body) made strenuous efforts to spread education, and succeeded in achieving much despite the limitations of their resources. The evangelical tours of Howell Harris, John Wesley, and Whitfield, all of whom laboured in Pembrokeshire for a time, were an important influence on the people, refining their mode of life, and directing their steps towards truer Christian witness.

The improvement in agriculture was due mainly to the interest of the landowners whose prosperity was indissolubly linked with the land. Enlightened landowners like Thomas Lloyd of Cwm-gloyn and Mirehouse of Brownslade, active land-agents like Thomas and Charles Hassall, were introducing new systems of farming, establishing better breeds of cattle, helping to form farmers' clubs, and writing essays and pamphlets on various aspects of the industry.

The acceleration of the Industrial Revolution led to greater productivity in Pembrokeshire coal mining, which was becoming a major industry, particularly in the Kilgetty-Saundersfoot area (where the Philippses of Picton Castle provided capital for further expansion), Hook, Freystrop, Landshipping, and Cresswell. Slate and stone quarrying was developed at Cilgerran, Llangolman, Rosebush, Porthgain, and later at Treffgarne. The quarries of Porthgain were near to the little cove which soon became a lively port with quay, storehouses, and cottages built for the quarrymen (Plate 31).

The founding of the Royal Dockyard, first at Milford, then at Pembroke Dock, and the founding of Milford as a fishing port by Charles Greville and Sir William Hamilton towards the end of the century, led to the development of the Haven, which in due course gave employment to thousands of people. Tenby, which had sunk into torpid gentility, suddenly came to life again, and through the exertions of Dr. Jones and Sir William Paxton became a fashionable resort for holidaymakers and for the ailing who sought relief from their ills in sea-bathing.

The annals of the eighteenth century are not complete without reference to the event known as "the landing of the French". In 1797 a force of some 1,400 men, which included a high percentage of jailbirds and other unsavoury characters, under command of General Tate, landed below Carreg Wastad, a small cove below the hamlet of Llanwnda. Before they could achieve any objective, a force of volunteers consisting of the Castlemartin Yeomanry, Fishguard Fencibles, and militia units, commanded by the energetic Lord Cawdor, marched against them, with the result that the enemy capitulated unconditionally. They were allowed to march to Goodwick Sands where they piled their arms. The landing caused great alarm throughout the land, and spurred the central government to expedite measures for the more effective protection of our shores. In the struggles with Napoleon, numerous Pembrokeshire men played a worthy part, chief among them General Sir Thomas Picton, of Poyston, who fell at Waterloo, leading his troops in repelling a desperate French attack.

Perhaps of all the periods in Pembrokeshire's history none was more important than the nineteenth century. It was an age of tremendous advance on the home front, politically and economically. Changes came fast and furious, generally to the good. The development of the coal industry and agricultural prosperity is again clearly reflected in the activity at the ports and the increasing seaborne trade. Haverfordwest and Tenby continued to be the main ports, but were closely rivalled by Milford Haven, Fishguard, even Solva. For instance, in 1837 there were 28 shipowners and 42 master mariners belonging to the port of Fishguard alone, and at one time some 200 vessels had landed cargoes at Solva. Among the shipowners of Fishguard in 1837 were merchants like Levi Vaughan, farmers like John Morgan Mortimer of Penysgwarne and Hugh Harries of Cefn-y-dre, and landowners like William Gwynne of Court. The market-house and the quay were improved and Fishguard became a flourishing town.

Land communications were reorganised when in 1850 the railroad came to the county and Neyland was selected as the terminus of the Great Western Railway. Accordingly, the packet station and the Irish trade were transferred from Milford to the new terminus, and a new town arose at Neyland. Ironically, the same causes that led to the little town's foundation and prosperity led also to its decline. In 1904–06 a harbour was constructed at Goodwick (on which the inappropriate name of Fishguard Harbour was bestowed), and soon superseded Neyland as the port for Ireland. It was now Goodwick's turn to prosper and grow from a sleepy hamlet into a bright little town, the only unimaginative intrusion being the newly erected "company houses" called Harbour Village.

A great improvement in road communications proved particularly helpful to the farming community. A slump occurred in agriculture in the late 1830s and in the 1840s, and this, together with other difficulties, led to outbreaks of violence known as the "Rebecca Riots". Farmers and workers assembled at nightfall, some disguised as women, and attacked and destroyed toll-gates and toll-houses, one of the main grievances being the excessive imposts levied on road-users. These outrages were suppressed only by bringing troops and extra police into the area. Fortunately, agriculture improved and more settled conditions resulted. A feature of this century is the formation of large numbers of farmers' societies and clubs, with the holding of cattle shows, ploughing matches, and other co-operative and competitive events.

Population statistics are usually a good guide to the state of a nation's prosperity, and become more obvious when studied at county level. In 1801 the population of this county was 56,280, which gradually increased until in 1861 it stood at 96,278, the highest figure it ever reached. By 1901 it had fallen to 87,894, partly through emigration of workers from the countryside to the industrial areas of Glamorgan where higher wages were the lure. Thereafter an appreciable increase occurred, and in 1921 there were 91,480 people in the county. During the depression between the two World Wars the population sank again, and by 1941 it had fallen to 85,400.

From the Act of Union of 1536 down to 1889, the county had been governed and administered by its ancient landowning families— Philipps of Picton Castle, Owen of Orielton, Edwardes and Tucker of Sealyham and Treffgarne, Lort of Stackpole, Barlow of Slebech, Bowen of Llwyngwair, Elliot of Narberth, Harries of Tregwynt, and a host more. Their services were voluntary and they held all the important appointments, "the levers of power", appointments like Lord Lieutenant, Deputy Lieutenants, High Sheriffs, Justices of the Peace, Members of Parliament, Clerks of the Peace, County Treasurer. Patronage lay entirely in their hands. Most important of all were the Justices of the Peace, who, through the Quarter Sessions, were responsible for the whole administration of the county. For over three and a half centuries the system had worked remarkably well, and it must be emphasised that the Justices were unpaid. Political and economic developments of the eighteenth and nineteenth centuries, the increase in population, and the growing complexities of administration made a change desirable, even necessary. What had done good service in 1580 was no longer effective to deal with the situation in 1880. The three great Reform Acts—1832, 1867, 1884— were the harbingers of the new era. Most significant of all was the Act passed in 1888 which reorganised local government and set up the machinery of county councils. It was a bell that tolled for the squires and marked the end of an age. Power now passed from the Justices of the Peace into the hands of the county council, whose members, drawn from all walks of life, were the elected representatives of the people. Henceforth the Quarter Sessions confined its work to legal matters. Thus from 1889 onwards the history of Pembrokeshire is largely that of its county, borough, and district councils, and to a lesser degree of the parish councils set up in 1894.

During the early part of the twentieth century Pembrokeshire life jogged on without any major changes. The second World War and its aftermath brought radical alterations. The advent of larger military and other government installations, the establishment of massive oil terminals on the shores of Milford Haven, the acceptance of the tourist trade as a source of income, the change from subsistence farming into a primarily profit-making industry, the production of turkeys on an immense scale, all helped to balance losses caused by the dwindling of the fishing industry at Milford, the closure of numerous railway installations, and the loss of the dockyard at Pembroke Dock. New faces, new skills, new attitudes, are transforming the way of life.

I conclude this review by reminding readers of the long literary tradition of the "premier county" of Wales. We start with Asser, bishop and scholar, a Pembrokeshire man who may have come from Trefaser in Pencaer, a friend of Alfred the Great. From Cemais came Dafydd ap Gwilym, one of the greatest poets of mediaeval Wales. Manorbier was the birthplace of Giraldus Cambrensis, "patron saint" of Pembrokeshire historians, whose *Itinerary* and *Works* are standard requirements for those who would unravel the mysteries of the twelfth century. Taking a long leap forward we come to George Owen, witty, gifted, provocative, who laid the basis of a study of our antiquities; and his son, also named George, who became York Herald of Arms; and his disciples, the Rev. George Owen Harry of Dinas, and George William Griffith of Penybenglog, skilled in the unravelling of genealogies and heraldic intricacies. In the eighteenth century Dr. Erasmus Saunders threw a vivid light on the condition of the see of St. David's, while the elegant prose of Richard Fenton of Glynymel has preserved much curious lore for our delectation; the poet Anna Williams of Rosemarket, friend of Dr. Johnson, the hymn-writer William Lewis of Abermawr, the Shakespearian commentator Maurice Morgan of Blaenbylan, were honoured by their contemporaries. Nearer our times we find Dr. Thomas Nicholas of Brawdy parish, secretary of the committee whose labours led to the establishment of the first university college of Wales, and author of *The County Families of Wales* and *Pedigree of the English People*; Edward Laws of Tenby, whose *Little England Beyond Wales* is essential reading for everyone interested in Pembrokeshire; and Romilly Allen, erudite antiquary and essayist. In the early part of the present century, a talented series of writers added their quota of publications, among them the Rev. Meredith Morris of Cwmgwaun; James Phillips of Haverfordwest; J. Rowland Phillips of Cilgerran; Dr. Henry Hicks and Francis Green, both of St. David's; Arthur Leach of Tenby; Principal David Salmon of Narberth; Sir Frederick Rees; Edgar Phillips (the Archdruid "Trefin"); Commander E. H. Stuart Jones; and the three gifted sons of Fishguard, the brothers T. H. Evans ("Igloo Habs"), the Rev. J. T. Evans, and the Rev. A. W. Wade Evans. Among those happily still with us, adding to their own reputation while providing literary delights for others, we can number Professor W. F. Grimes, Dr. B. G. Charles, B. G. Owens, Dr. Brian Howells, Dr. David Howell, Dillwyn Miles, Stanley Richards, and Douglas James. All these writers have been inspired by the land that gave them birth and have given back to Pembrokeshire, in generous measure, sparkling gems polished by intellectual qualities which many envy and which all acclaim.

8

Industrial Archaeology

by ROBERT A. KENNEDY

THERE are many fine examples of the blacksmith's craft in **Pembroke**-shire. Most evident are the gates and railings which survived the scrap drive of the last war. Many gates fill older and narrower field entrances, indicating by their width the earlier stage in the development of the agricultural industry before machinery—and the industry which produced it—took the labour from the land in the wake of the Industrial Revolution. The small gates and railings bounding residential property are well worth studying. Along with wrought iron work of high quality there is also a profusion of cast iron work and frequently the two are combined, as in the wrought framework which supports the cast decorative units embellishing a fine terraced town house in Spring Gardens, Haverfordwest.

Where did all the fine cast iron railings of Tenby and Milford Haven, Haverfordwest, Narberth, Fishguard, and Newport come from? And where was the iron itself obtained? True, Pembrokeshire's extensive sea-trade imported numerous examples; like the *art nouveau* cast railings in front of the Old Printing House, Solva. But many examples were cast in the county and even exported beyond its borders. The Woodside Foundry, near Tenby, seems to have specialised in work of this kind. There were numerous "forges" and foundries, and an excellent example actually survives at Milford Docks.

The continuity and close relationship between craft and industry in iron is seldom properly appreciated. It is hardly better demonstrated than in Pembrokeshire. It is also not sufficiently appreciated that the Industrial Revolution started in the rural areas of Britain. This region possessed great mineral wealth, apart from iron which, like the coal, was exploited from prehistoric (Iron Age) times. The advent of the Industrial Revolution in the county, as in other rural areas, was due to availability of timber and therefore of charcoal for the early furnaces, and because water was the main source of power, while labour (which depended upon the distribution of the population) was still mainly rural. By modern standards towns were small and were commercial centres serving the surrounding rural areas.

This is not to say that manufacturing industry was non-existent before the growth of "heavy" industry—far from it. But the concerns were relatively small, widely scattered, and like the other commercial enterprises were closely linked to the self-sufficient economy of their area. Chief among these rural manufactures was the woollen industry. Of over 30 woollen mills still working in Pembrokeshire[1] at the beginning of this century, three survive today. Those at Tregwynt (895349) and Wallis (014258) are well worth a visit, for there can be seen the "Spinning Mule", an invention originating in 1779. The third, at Middle Mill, Solva (807259), now specialises in weaving carpets, though these are still based upon the traditional and complex Welsh "tapestry" designs.

The essentially rural industries are not our main concern here, for they were not part of the Industrial Revolution, though later affected by it through the inventions and mechanisation which followed. It would be wrong to overlook the "grist" mills, many of which still contain their machinery, often entirely of wood and of exceptional interest to the specialist. Outstanding examples were Blackpool (Plate 30), Llawhaden, and the tidal mills of Pembroke and Carew, the last surviving complete and in a setting of exceptional beauty.

Another extensive and vital rural industry yet to receive detailed attention by the historian is that of lime production.[2] Throughout the county are numerous lime kilns, like the fine group of round ones at Solva (Plate 32), or the great square one at Caerbwdi, near St. David's. Here again we have the association between craft and industry in the ancient crafts of lime burning and of quarrying. The county possessed a great quarrying industry, supplying the limestone to be burnt in the kilns for agriculture and for mortar, or for use as building stone. Transport of the limestone was largely by the prolific coastal traffic maintained by wooden ketches and schooners. Many of these were built locally and examples lie as hulks at Angle, south of the Haven.

In this peninsular region almost everything was carried round the coast to the many small ports and deep into the heart of the county at Haverfordwest. The Western Cleddau was navigable by substantial cargo vessels, and for this reason the town became the greatest inland seaport in Wales. Fortunately enough evidence of this still survives, including some fine warehouses and the original Custom House on the Old Quay, built of limestone from the great quarries at West Williamston. One outstanding example of Haverfordwest's importance is the extent of the paper-making industry during the eighteenth and nineteenth centuries. Five paper mills existed around the town, all water-powered; the most important example of them still survives in a ruinous state at Prendergast.

It was by sea that the high-quality Pembrokeshire anthracite was exported in earlier times (before the final closure of the industry by the National Coal Board in 1947). It is hard now to believe that, from such coastal collieries as those at Newgale and Nolton, vessels powered only by sail were loaded at anchor, only a few yards off what is still one of the most dangerous coasts in Britain. A few of the iron rings and mooring stanchions may be seen from the coastal footpath. Like sea trading,[3] the coal industry has a great story yet to be told in full.[4] The county was extensively mined. At Hook, small private pits were still being worked by mediaeval techniques into the twentieth century. On the other hand, in the mid-nineteenth century at the magnificent complex at Stepaside—where the superb buildings still stand (Plate 33)—the Grove Pit in the woods above "yielded coal of the highest quality",[5] and a little later supplied the great ironworks in the valley below. Across the valley, iron mines provided the ore while a system of tramways and also a canal served the foundry and carried the products to the coast for shipment. The original main tramway consisted of "fish-belly" rails laid on stone sleeper blocks, which are still to be seen. A branch of the line passed through its own separate arch beneath the present road bridge (A 477), reputedly built by Thomas Telford. This part of southern Pembrokeshire was once extensively intersected by industrial tramways, and all the types from those with wooden rails to the later "bridge-back" and finally the T-head types were represented.

Other important foundries were at Neyland, which produced kitchen ranges; Blackpool, a subsidiary "forge" or furnace of the great ironworks at Carmarthen; and the old Marychurch ironworks at Haverfordwest, which earned gold and silver medals for the agricultural machinery it produced during the second half of the nineteenth century. It was situated between the river and Bridge Street. After a change of ownership it finally stopped production when the boilers burst, showering the town with bricks.

The Penygored Tinplate Works, situated in the north of the county beside the river Teifi, near Llechryd, is an outstanding example of an early industry (started *c.* 1765) in a deeply rural setting. A great fortune was expended upon this enterprise, of which the canal and two superb bridges—the Hammett Bridge and the Castle Maelgwyn Bridge—and remains of the works can still be seen. The works employed up to 300 men, but unfortunately its isolation from the sources of raw materials, which were imported by water via Cardigan, led to its closure in 1806.

Nearby and below the fine castle at Cilgerran was a noted slate quarry. The towpath used by the bargees who conveyed the slate still exists. Several varieties of high-quality slate were produced by quarries in the county, notably at Abereiddi, where the tramway can still be seen following the contour round inland to Porthgain Harbour; at Rosebush, and from the Maenclochog area, whence came the distinctive Presely slate which roofed the Houses of Parliament at Westminster. The geology of the county is so varied that justice cannot be done here to the quarrying industry. Nor is there space to deal adequately with the county's unique railway history.[6] But for the enthusiast, in spite of progressive closures and recent nationalised vandalism by demolition of the beautiful 1853–56 station architecture, there is much to discover. Fishguard Harbour was to be the terminus of Isambard Kingdom Brunel's broad-gauge Atmospheric railway; this, however, was never completed, though remains of the workings can be seen in Treffgarne gorge to the south. The present link with the Irish Sea traffic was not completed until 1906, when Fishguard took over from New Milford (Neyland).

The mineral wealth of the county was greater than it appears today. The ruins of the lead and silver mine at Llanfyrnach are a monument to the extraction of non-ferrous metals. A gold mine is reputed to have existed in Treffgarne gorge. And quite extensive copper deposits, now apparently exhausted, were mined along the southern coast of the St. David's peninsula. Little remains of these workings now, but the presence of copper may be significant in view of the evident importance of the region in Bronze Age times.

It may be as well to close with a note of warning. Many sites are unsuitable for the casual visitor and particularly for children. Nearly all are somewhat ruinous, while the mines and quarries should be viewed with great care. The numerous "drift" levels exposed along the coast in the Newgale, Nolton, and Broad Haven areas are best not explored unless under the direction of a trained speleologist. On the other hand, for the experienced visitor there is rewarding work to be done in the county. Comprehensive research into our industrial history has only recently been initiated by the Field Studies Centres and the County Museum. For the serious enthusiast who wishes to combine study with holidays there is ample scope.

References

[1] Pembrokeshire and the Woollen Industry, *The Pembrokeshire Historian*, No. 2, 1966, pp. 48–53, by J. Geraint Jenkins.

[2] Pembrokeshire Sea Trading Before 1900, *Field Studies*, Vol. 2, 1, 1964, by Barbara J. George.

[3] *Ibid.*

[4] The Coal Industry in Pembrokeshire, *Field Studies*, Vol. 1, 5, 1963, by George Edwards.

[5] *Ibid.*

[6] *The Saundersfoot Railway* and *The North Pembrokeshire Railway*, published by the Oakwood Press.

PLATE 37.   A quiet sail at Newport

PLATE 38.   Gliding at Withybush

9

The Park Planning Authority

by J. A. PRICE

Administration. The Pembrokeshire Coast National Park has an area of 225 square miles and the smallest land-mass of the ten National Parks that have so far been established. It is divided into four distinct sectors: the South Pembrokeshire coast; the St. Bride's Bay—Strumble Head sector; North Pembrokeshire, including the Presely Hills; and the Daugleddau sector. The Park lies wholly within the one county and is administered by the Pembrokeshire National Park Committee, to whom the county council has delegated most of its responsibilities for administration under the National Parks and Access to the Countryside Act of 1949, the Countryside Act of 1968, and the various Town and Country Planning Acts.

That Act of 1949 placed on National Parks Authorities a twofold duty: to preserve and enhance the natural beauty of the area designated, and to promote the enjoyment of the Park by the public. Development is carefully controlled with these factors in mind through the active use of general planning powers. The National Park Committee has eighteen members, two-thirds of whom are members of the county council and one-third appointed by the Secretary of State for Wales for their specialised knowledge.

Preservation and enhancement of the landscape. The National Park Committee, through its plans sub-committee, considers applications requiring planning consent and seeks to ensure that, as far as possible, new buildings, alterations to existing buildings, overhead electricity lines, and the various changes of land use, including camping and caravan sites, are carried out so as to cause the least possible injury to the landscape. Numerous tree preservation orders have been made and the Authority works in close consultation with the Forestry Commission upon the rehabilitation of existing woodlands and the afforestation of other lands. With the rising popularity of Pembrokeshire as a holiday area, pressure of development has mounted in the past decade, and the Park Authority finds difficulty in reconciling the need to accommodate visitors with the fundamental requirement of conserving the landscape.

The development over the past ten years of the Milford Haven Waterway as a major European port has presented a serious challenge to the National Park Authority, as part of the area lies within the Park. Vast works resulting from these activities have made impact on the landscape. These works comprise three major refineries (a fourth is now under construction), one of Europe's largest oil-fired power stations, and an oil terminal to serve an existing refinery at Swansea. A conservative estimate of the cost of these works is £200 million.

At the inception of development of the port the local planning authority sought to contain it within the middle reaches of the waterway extending from Sandy Haven to Burton on the north shore and from Popton Point to Cosheston on the south shore. (Apart from a proposal to establish a large iron ore stockpiling area on the Angle peninsula, an idea vigorously opposed by the Park Authority and later abandoned, all these major works have been confined within the area designated by the Authority.) In all cases the Park Authority sought, and obtained, the agreement of developers to the employment of a landscape consultant; and, under the expert guidance of the late S. Colwyn Foulkes, the lay-out and siting of works were modified so as to ensure the maximum consideration for landscape conservation and the most careful regard to the visual impact of these vast projects on their surroundings. As far as practicable, existing landscape features have been fully used, for example, by siting works in valleys and folds and away from the high lands, with judicious choice of colouring for oil tanks and other structures. It is considered that the development of the Milford Haven Waterway illustrates how vast industrial enterprises can be integrated with reasonable success into a landscape of special scenic character. On the other hand, the scale of these developments is such that their impact has been fundamental. The most disturbing features to those concerned with landscape conservation are sections of the 400-kV grid lines which have been necessary to link the Pembroke power station with areas to the east. These duplicate lines, however, have been routed to avoid the National Park.

One of the more serious problems facing the National Park Committee on the designation of the Park in 1952 was the disfigurement of landscape caused by numerous derelict Armed Service establishments abandoned after the war. There were four airfields, a wireless station, and many camps and isolated buildings. The National Park Authority sought, through various agencies, to remove these eyesores, and work has been undertaken by the Authority itself, by volunteers whom it organised, by the Armed Services and by other agencies, so that a considerable part of the dereliction has been removed; but there is still far too much evidence of unfortunate blemishes, and the problem of their clearance still causes grave concern to the committee.

Promotion of enjoyment by the public. Of the national parks in Wales, the Pembrokeshire Coast probably offers as wide a range of attractions for open-air recreation as any, ranging from boating and sailing to rock climbing and gliding. It has fine beaches, a superb inland waterway, historic buildings and sites, nature reserves, and nearly every type of countryside pursuit. Apart from the Tenby-Saundersfoot area, the Park does not receive a heavy influx of day visitors; most people wishing to enjoy its beauties do so by seeking accommodation in or around the Park. Whereas in 1949 there was accommodation for approximately 14,000 resident visitors in Pembrokeshire, this number had increased by 1971 to some 60,000. With improved highways, and particularly with the completion of the Severn Bridge, it is anticipated that this upward trend will continue. The Park Authority seeks to permit the expansion of tourist accommodation in appropriate locations whilst vigorously opposing development of areas where scenic quality would depreciate through such activities.

The Countryside Commission (formerly the National Parks Commission) engaged consultants to advise on the future needs of this Park in accommodation, and, as a result of their deliberations, a policy has been established under which it is intended to resist further development in the more "remote" parts but to build up small holiday resorts at Freshwater East on the south coast and at Broad Haven on the west coast.

A further problem causing concern to the Park Authority is the control of camping and caravanning. It is appreciated that this type of accommodation is essential in order to put up the increasing numbers of people visiting the Park. Consents for the siting of approximately 1,300 caravans had been issued by 1959, but by 1971 the number was 9,488, of which 7,591 were on site during the first week of August. Most of the sites are used seasonally or on long letting. To accommodate the genuine touring caravanner, the Park Authority is operating a site for this purpose at Sageston, Carew, and intends to develop a further transit caravan site at Kilgetty, near Tenby.

So that visitors may enjoy the beauty of the Park, car parks and roadside lay-bys have been constructed and the Authority has an extensive programme for more of both. Four full-time wardens and a large body of voluntary wardens are ready and willing to help visitors with information about the Park.

One of the most interesting features of the Park is the long-distance footpath extending around the Pembrokeshire Coast for a distance of 167 miles, a route which has been open in entirety since 1970.

Information services. Information centres exist at the Tenby Civic Centre; the County Museum at Haverfordwest; the City Hall at St. David's; the Town Hall at Fishguard; and adjoining the castle at Pembroke. The Tenby and Haverfordwest centres are open throughout the year; the St. David's and Pembroke centres from Easter to the end of September. A wide range of information on the Park available includes maps, photographs, exhibits, pamphlets and other publications, and the staff at the centres will readily assist visitors. The Park Planning Authority has published an official guide-book to Pembrokeshire, a register of holiday accommodation, and numerous information sheets, brochures, and leaflets.

The Countryside Commission established the Pembrokeshire Countryside Unit under the direction of John H. Barrett, who has arranged each summer a series of conducted tours, walks, and lectures at various locations throughout the Park. The Unit has its base at Broad Haven on St. Bride's Bay, in a specially designed building which has an exhibition and lecture hall.

Additional information on any aspect of the Park may be obtained from the County Offices, Haverfordwest.

The symbol of a razorbill defines the boundaries of the Park and is used on all forms of publicity.

10

Some Places of Interest

ABERCUCH (248409) was the home of a long line of wood turners whose tools were derived from those used by Celts on Lake Neuchâtel during the Early Iron Age. The coracles used by the local fishermen are just as old. Cwm Cuch, up the valley, is the locale of the first tale of *Y Mabinogi*, the oldest Welsh saga extant; it was here that Pwyll, Prince of Dyfed, chose to go and hunt, and here he met the King of the Other World. A coypu caught in the garden opposite the Nag's Head in 1949 is the only one recorded in West Wales.

AMBLESTON (001259), *Treamlod* in Welsh, is a village grouped around a church that is completely rebuilt except for its Norman tower. Its font, once sold to a churchwarden and used as a cheese-press and a pig-trough, is restored. The most important Roman settlement in Pembrokeshire stood at Castle Flemish (007267) and consists of an irregular quadrilateral containing a building and defended by a rampart and ditch; this was probably a small fort or military post designed to guard the forward lines of communication and occupied from the first half of the second century A.D. In a field at Scollock West Farm is a modern white marble monument to John and Mary Llewellin who "by the blessing of God on their joint undertaking and thrift . . . bought this farm and handed it down without encumbrances to their heirs". Woodstock Chapel (022257) was built in 1754 and was the first Methodist chapel not to be consecrated by a bishop.

AMROTH (163079) is a seaside village overlooking a beach that was once the hunting ground of some of the earliest men to reach these shores; ebonised stumps mark the remains of the sunken forest where they left flint flakes and cores used in the chase, and stags' horns and fossilised hazel nuts. An earthwork near Trelissey Farm consists of two concentric banks containing a rectangular building which was occupied from the second to the fourth centuries and was probably, like Castle Flemish at Ambleston, a small military outpost designed as a forward salient. Amroth Castle is a nineteenth-century house; nearby is a mound that may have been the site of the Castle of Earwere, the Norse name for the place. Wiseman's Bridge

(Andrew Wiseman held land there in 1324) was chosen for the rehearsal in 1943 for the Normandy invasion under the eagle eye of Winston Churchill. Colby Lodge, hidden in a deep wooded valley north of the village, was designed by John Nash.

ANGLE (865030) has evidence of a Neolithic settlement in the Devil's Quoit, a burial chamber standing on Broomhill Burrows beside the ridgeway that traversed the whole length of South Pembrokeshire, and of the Iron Age in the promontory forts at Castle Bay and West Pickard camps. The village, of a feudal pattern, has an odd assortment of antiquities. A tradition has it that three co-heiresses built each of them a house: one built the castle of which a pele-tower remains, and a dovecote with a domed roof as a manorial memento; the second built a house with pointed stone windows to the south-west of the churchyard; and the third erected the Hall. The tiny Fisherman's Chapel in the churchyard was raised above a crypt in 1447 and has a stained glass window showing Christ walking on Gennesaret. The single street is lined with colour-washed cottages, pink and yellow and plumbago blue, and the Globe Hotel, in fine colonial style. West Angle Bay has a sandy beach; beyond it is Thorn Island with its nineteenth-century fort converted into an hotel. Popton Fort has been cleverly disguised as the offices of the BP tanker terminal.

BEGELLY (118075). A scattered village 5 miles north of Tenby; probably a corruption of the Welsh name *Bugeildy* (the shepherds' house). The tall church tower with corner pinnacles served as a watch tower in the last war. In the house behind it, Augustus John spent much time as a boy, and on Kingsmoor Common below, he saw gipsies. So many coal-pits were opened at Begelly in the sixteenth century that the main road was threatened with subsidence and carriages to Tenby dared not pass.

BONCATH (205384) is Welsh for buzzard; it stands on a cross-roads and is surrounded by many mansion-houses. Ffynhonnau was designed by John Nash in 1792 for John Colby, who commanded the Royal Pembrokeshire Militia and helped to raise the alarm when the French landed near Fishguard in 1797; and although the house was remodelled by Inigo Thomas in 1904, the elegant interior is original. Newchapel, nearby, was built for those who served the gentry. Cilwendeg, now an old people's home, is a Georgian house built by Morgan Jones, a retiring gentleman who derived a huge income from the Skerry lighthouse off Anglesey. An early nineteenth-century grotto has shell-lined walls and an intricate flooring. Boncath is partly in the parish of Capel Colman, said to be named after the Irish saint Colman of Dromore; Maen Colman is an inscribed stone of about the seventh century. The church, dedicated to the same saint, was rebuilt in 1835 and restored at the end of the last century; in 1721 it was ruinous, a "solitary habitation of owls and jackdaws".

BOSHERSTON (966948), or Stackpole Bosher as it was called in the thirteenth century, is famous for its dragon-flied, water-lilied ponds and for its mere. Boshersmere (963929), said George Owen, is one of "ye divers wonders of Pembrokeshire"; from its two blowholes, connected underground, spouts shoot 40 feet into the air in a sou'-westerly gale. Bosherston Pools are three streams blocked by sandbars, once believed to be the waters out of which the hand reached for King Arthur's sword, Excalibur; they provide good pike fishing (see *Hook, Line and Spinner* by Clive Gammon). St. Govan's Chapel (Plate 21), deep in a cleft in the cliffs below Trevalen (*recté* Trefalun) Downs, was once believed to have been the cell of St. Gawaine who turned hermit and hid in a niche by the altar, in which the visitor may turn and wish a wish. Its empty bellcote held a silver bell which was stolen by pirates; a tempest rose and sank their ship, but sea-nymphs rescued the bell and placed it beside the holy well, between the chapel and the sea, entombed in a rock that rings out on being struck. The parish church of St. Michael has two effigies and a churchyard cross bearing a head of Christ at the intersection, all probably of the fourteenth century. Great walls of limestone cliffs stretch to east and west. A huntsman once leapt over a chasm in these cliffs and dropped dead when he looked back, hence Huntsman's Leap (961929). Broad Haven (978940) has a golden beach which must be approached by scrambling down a slope.

> (*This area is closed for firing practice on the Castlemartin ranges at times announced in the local Press and at Bosherston post office.*)

BRIDELL (176420) has an ogam stone in its churchyard inscribed to the memory of Nettasagrus, son of the son of Brecos, who lived in the sixth century. Plas y Bridell is now a Carmelite convent. The composer of the famous Welsh hymn "Calon Lân" was born in the parish.

BROAD HAVEN (861135), on the coast of St. Bride's Bay, with its extensive sandy beach, became fashionable as a bathing place at the beginning of the nineteenth century. The main road is its promenade and there is a large car park in which the Pembrokeshire Countryside Unit stands. Evidence of the Coal Measures of the Pembrokeshire beds are to be seen in the spectacularly folded cliffs.

BURTON (985054) is a popular yachting centre: *Le Gift of God of Burton* sailed from here in 1566. A burial chamber known as the Hanging Stone (972082) is probably a passage-grave site. Benton Castle's white tower peering from the trees above the river is a recent reconstruction by Ernest Pegge, built with his own hands and with his own death mask over the door; it was originally put up to guard the pills and upper reaches of the Cleddau. The church is a mile inland and is largely fourteenth-century, with lancet windows which may have belonged to an earlier edifice. An altar tomb of about 1520 bears the arms of the Wogans of Boulston. Its name indicates that Burton was a fortified settlement.

CALDEY (140965) was called *Ynys Pŷr* by the Welsh—the island of Pŷr, whose manor was at Manorbier—long before the Norse named it Caldey, "cold island". There were monks here before St. Columba went to Iona and it may be that Pyr was their first abbot; he was succeeded by Samson early in the sixth century. An inscribed monument of that century commemorates one Maglia-Dubracunas; another, of the ninth century, reads: "And by the sign of the Cross (which) I have fashioned upon that (stone) I ask all who walk here that they pray for the soul of Cadwgan." In the same century, the Norse destroyed the monastery. The island was granted to the Benedictine monks of St. Dogmael's Abbey early in the twelfth century and Robert Martin, lord of Cemais, established a priory there. After the Dissolution, Caldey was purchased by John Bradshaw and it passed through various ownerships before it was bought, in 1897, by the Rev. Donne Bushell, a chaplain of Harrow, who began to repair the monastic buildings. In 1906 an Anglican community settled there and established the abbey church; they entered the Roman Catholic order of Benedictines in 1913 and dedicated the church to St. Samson, some of whose relics were sent from the cathedral at Dol, in Brittany. The Benedictines went to Prinknash in 1929 and monks of the Cistercian Order of Strict Observance came from Chimay, in Belgium, in their place.

Nanna's Cave was occupied successively by Palaeolithic, Neolithic, Bronze Age, and Iron Age peoples and during the Romano-British era. The large quantity of animal bones found in the cave indicates that Caldey was then a low hill peering out of Coedrath Forest. Later, oyster beds lay where the forest was. In Elizabethan times the islanders kept no oxen for fear of pirates. Paul Jones has left his name on a bay, after an alleged visit, and his ghost stalks the cliffs on moonless nights.

Boats leave from Tenby Harbour at regular times. The monks farm the island and manufacture perfume. There is a post office and tea-rooms.

CAMROSE (927202) is a hamlet half-hidden in a valley, most famous as the home of the Berry family. The second son took the name of the parish when he was elevated to the peerage; the others called themselves Barons Kemsley and Buckland on their elevation. Keeston Castle is an earthwork, consisting of three concentric lines of defence: its Welsh name, *Tregetin*, is a reminder that the original name was Ketingston. The parish church, dedicated to St. Ishmael, was restored in 1883; the tower is battlemented and has a polygonal turret and a gaily painted weathercock. There may have been a chapel at St. Catherine's Bridge.

CAREW (048037) may be a corruption of the Welsh *caerau* (forts): the local people call it Carey. Carew Beacon is a burial mound on the Ridgeway which was converted into a beacon in 1803 to warn against invasion; other mounds flank Rosemary Lane. Carew Cross is a fine early Christian monument covered with interlaced decoration and an inscription in insular majuscule commemorating "Maredudd the king, son of Edwin", great-grandson of Hywel Dda, who was slain in battle in 1035. Carew Castle (Plate 28) was founded probably by Gerald de Windsor, castellan of Pembroke; some say he got it as part of the dowry of his famous wife, Nest, "the Helen of Wales". His descendant mortgaged it to Sir Rhys ap Thomas, who held a magnificent tournament within its walls in 1507, and, on the impeachment of his grandson, the castle passed to Sir John Perrott, Lord Deputy of Ireland and reputed son of Henry VIII. Sir John installed piped water and furnished the place with damasks and books and all manner of musical instruments, but before he could enjoy them he was tried for treason and died attainted in the Tower. During the Civil Wars Carew Castle suffered two sieges and damage from which it never recovered. It has long mused, Narcissus-like, upon its own lovely reflection in the still waters of the high tide. (Guide-book available at the castle.) The parish church at Carew Cheriton has a corner steeple and contains tombs and effigies of the Carew family which are duplicated in Camerton Church, Somerset. A chantry chapel in the church-yard, once an ossuary, was used as a school and as a home for paupers. Carew mill is tidal, often known as a French mill; it has been renovated and restored by the National Park Committee.

CASTLEMARTIN (915983) began as a "rath", an earthwork of Irish origin, and, although it was the head of a manor, it never became more than a stockaded enclosure; there is no trace of a Norman castle or fortified manor house. Early stone implements and pottery found in the sand-dunes nearby indicate prehistoric settlement in this part of the county, and the early forts at Linney Head, Flimston Castle, and Bulliber were occupied in Roman times. The parish church is dedicated to St. Michael. Its floor rises in steps towards the chancel, which is dug into the rising ground, where stand the ruins of a building of unknown but ancient origin, known as the Old Rectory. The organ once belonged to Mendelssohn and found its way to Castlemartin from Suffolk through a local family connexion. Flimston Chapel (924956), dedicated to St. Martin, was used as a barn until it was restored in 1903. Ermigate Cross, by the side of the road leading to the chapel, was reconsecrated in 1963. The Castlemartin Black Cattle derive from the "horned, coal-black Pembrokeshire cattle". They were improved by that agricultural pioneer John Mirehouse, of Brownslade, and they had their own herd book in 1874 but were later merged in the Welsh Blacks.

Eligug Stack (926944) (Plate 5), a jagged tooth of lime-stone crowned with guillemots in summer, retains the almost forgotten Welsh name for those birds. Razorbills and kittiwakes also nest there and it has a thick growth of tree-mallow. The Green Bridge of Wales is an incredible arch of fine proportions jutting out of the immense wall of Carboni-ferous Limestone cliffs reaching from Linney Head to St. Govan's.

CILGERRAN (194430) has a castle that has been portrayed by Richard Wilson (National Museum of Wales) and J. M. W. Turner (Tate Gallery), and has inspired poets. It was built in 1093 by Roger, Earl of Montgomery, high above the tidal limit of the Teifi so that it is unassailable from the west and north. Two great drum towers (Plate 26) and a gatehouse of slate defend it on the landward, but it was taken by the Welsh time and again. The Ministry of Public Building and Works has restored it and has provided an official guide-book. Cilgerran was a borough governed by a Portreeve and Corporation until 1882. It was the birthplace of John Rowland Phillips, the antiquary, who wrote *The History of Cilgerran* (1867); and Thomas Phaer, physician to Mary I and translator of Virgil's *Aeneid*, lived nearby. In the churchyard is a stone inscribed in Latin and in ogam to the memory of Trenegussus, son of Macutrenus, who died in the sixth century. Coracles race (Plate 25) each August in the gorge, which is a great place for salmon. A net across the river was connected to a bell in Coedmor, the house in the trees above, in the old days.

COSHESTON (004037) is a secluded village gay with colour-washed cottages above a creek in the Haven. Nearby is Upton Castle built by the Malefants in the thirteenth century, but nothing remains beyond a gateway and flanking towers. A private chapel in the grounds has tombs bearing effigies of early Malefants, a fine Norman font, and a Jacobean pulpit brought from St. Mary's Church, Haverfordwest.

CRYMYCH (184339) was a farmhouse until the railway came and converted it into a busy agricultural centre; this it remains even though the railway has been taken away. The road from Cardigan to Tenby crosses the prehistoric ridgeway above which, to the west, stands Moel Drygarn with its thrice-crowned hill-fort (Plate 18) and, to the east, Y Freni Fawr where, it is said, the Roman Emperor Magnus Maximus came to hunt and left his name on its summit, Cadair Facsen, the chair of Maximus.

DALE (810058). Robert de Vale received a grant of a weekly market, and a fair on 14 September annually, in 1293 at his "manor of Dale". Dale Castle probably stands on the site of his strong-hold. The stone that marked the site of the martyrdom of William Nichol at Haverfordwest in 1558 is now in the castle grounds. At sunset on Sunday, 7 August 1485, Henry Tudor landed at Mill Bay to begin his march to Bosworth Field and the crown of England. There are Iron Age promontory forts at Great Castle Head and Dale Point, where, in a nineteenth-century fort, is the Dale Fort Field Centre. St. Ann's Head lighthouse is built on the site of St. Ann's Chapel, a ruin by the time of Elizabeth I. Dale is the sunniest place in Wales and, with its fertile soil, produces early crops of potatoes. It is a busy sailing centre.

DINAS (012389), Welsh for "little fortress", has a promontory fort at Castell (004382), but a Neolithic axehead found at Cwmyreglwys may indicate earlier settlement. The headland was once cut off by the sea and retains the memory in its name, formerly Ynys Fach Llyffan Gawr, the islet of Llyffan the Giant. It is the locale of R. M. Lockley's *Island Farmers* and *Golden Year*. Brynhenllan, "the old church-hill", may have been the site of an early church. The church at Cwmyreglwys, "the valley of the church", was destroyed by the great storm of October 1859 which sank the *Royal Charter* and 113 other ships off the Welsh coast. The present church was built in the following year for £789, and is dedicated to St. Brynach. Cwmyreglwys is one of the loveliest coves in Wales; from it a path leads to Pwllgwaelod, another secluded bay with a lime kiln and an inn that belong to the coastal trading days. A footpath encircles Dinas Island where feral goats clung to the slopes until they were destroyed in 1947; grey seals breed in the caves below. Strange depressions on a slab of rock at Dinas Head were pronounced to be the devil's footprints. The fairies *Bendith y Mamau* had their city here under the sea and once, when a Dinas fisherman cast anchor, a little man came up the rope and complained that the anchor had gone through his roof!

EGLWYSWRW (142385), the church of St. Wrw, a virgin saint whose body lay in a tomb in a transeptal chapel; corpses that were buried in it in mediaeval times were "cast out of the said chapel in the night tyme" and therefore the parishioners "held opinion that their holie saint will not have any bedfellows". Eglwyswrw was one of the twenty knights' fees of the barony of Cemais; its Court Leet still meets, largely to allocate sheep ear-marks. An armoury for the trained bands of the barony was built near the church before 1600. The Court, a moated manor house "both of account and strength", was the home of David Martin (d. 1327), Bishop of St. David's and lord of Eglwyswrw. Chess was played in the village in mediaeval times. Parnassus School, "a classical and commercial seminary", taught stenography in four lessons and tradesmen's arithmetic in six at a fee of 35p. St. Meugan's Fair is held in the village on the Monday after Martinmas. St. Meugan's Well gave forth three kinds of water, to heal warts, sore eyes, and heart disease.

FISHGUARD (958370) is a sheltered harbour; the monuments of those who sought its shelter 4,000 years ago surround the bay. Its Welsh name, *Abergwaun*, derives from its situation at the estuary of the river Gwaun; its other name is Scandinavian for a fish-yard. Fishguard people used to live by catching herrings and by curing and exporting pilchards. The manor of Fishguard, "villa" and "patria", was part of the barony of Cemais and was granted to John Bradshaw, of St. Dogmael's, at the Dissolution, but it was later bought by a gentleman in "the hamlet of Cavendish Square, W.1". The last invasion of Britain took place here in 1797 when three French men-of-war and a lugger landed the *Légion Noire*, 600 troops and 800 ex-convicts, under a renegade Irish-American, William Tate, at Carreg Wastad (927406). The half-starved invaders succumbed to the sucking pigs and poultry of Pencaer and to the liquor stacked in every farm and cottage after a recent wreck, so that they easily mistook the Welsh women in their red shawls for Grenadiers (who, incidentally, wore blue in those days) arriving as reinforcements for Lord Cawdor's Pembroke Yeomanry, and they surrendered their arms on Goodwick Sands. The Pembroke Yeomanry has ever since worn *Fishguard* as a battle honour, the only one ever won on British soil. A memorial in St. Mary's churchyard commemorates Jemima Nicholas who, armed with a pitchfork, captured a dozen Frenchmen. Eighteen years earlier Paul Jones is said to have fired two broadsides on the town and demanded 500 guineas; he maimed Mary Fenton and got the money. Mary's brother, Richard Fenton, was a friend of Goldsmith, Garrick, Burke, Reynolds, and Dr. Johnson, and author of *A Historical Tour through Pembrokeshire* (1810). Fishguard Harbour, blasted out of the cliff in 1906 to receive the "greyhounds of the Atlantic", is the terminus of the cross-channel service to Rosslare. Lower Fishguard, the old port, is a growing sailing centre.

FRESHWATER EAST (019984) has a large sandy beach backed by sand-dunes and flanked by red sandstone cliffs, but there is a spread of chalets and caravans and plans are in hand to develop the place as a holiday village.

FRESHWATER WEST (885990) is a 4-mile stretch of golden sand and low rocks, but the sea is unsafe for bathing. Sand blown from the shore at low tide has formed extensive dunes which have covered several Bronze Age burials and surround the Devil's Quoit, a New Stone Age burial chamber. A Mesolithic site recently excavated at Little Furzenip Quarry (886994) revealed 7,700 flints. A dragon-embossed tablet found on the beach is probably Scandinavian. Gupton, nearby, is named after Cybi ab Erbin who lived in the ninth century. A 1914–18 calvary stands over the bay.

GRASSHOLM (598093) is the outermost of the offshore islands and can be reached only when wind and tide permit. A colony of 15,000 pairs of gannets breeding on the island provide one of the most magnificent sights in nature. There are evidences of a prehistoric settlement.

GUMFRESTON Church (110011) has paintings on the north wall of its nave and a pre-Reformation sanctus bell. Ships went up the Ritec as far as Gumfreston at high tide in the old days. Scotsborough House, now a ruin, was the home of the Perrotts from about 1300 to 1614 and then of the descendants of Sir Rhys ap Thomas. Daisyback was the home of the ancestors of Benjamin Hall, Lord Llanover, who gave his name to Big Ben.

GWAUN VALLEY (030340) winds delightfully from Newport to Fishguard. Along its length are the churches of Cilgwyn, Pontfaen, Llanychllwydog, Llanllawer, and Llanychaer. Near Llanllawer is Parc y Meirw (Field of the Dead) which contains the largest megalithic alignment in Wales; it is over 140 feet in length and four of its eight pillars are still standing; a lady in white is said to walk among them on dark nights. The valley is long held to have been the home of "ghoulies and ghosties" and it still has a fey quality. The people cling to old customs and celebrate the New Year according to the Gregorian calendar on 13 January.

HAVERFORDWEST (955155) is the county town, from which roads radiate to all parts. Its name is English, derived from *haefer*, meaning a he-goat or buck; that is, the ford used by goats. On the commanding foreland overlooking this, the lowest ford on the Western Cleddau, Gilbert de Clare, lord of Pembroke, built a castle some time before 1120. A garrison town grew in the shadow of the castle and traces of its walls are to be found in gardens and back-yards. There was a strong Flemish element in the town in mediaeval times. Gruffydd ap Rhys captured it after the battle of Cardigan in 1136; Llywelyn the Great burnt it up to the castle walls in 1220; and Owain Glyndwr besieged it in 1405. The town changed hands during the Civil Wars; it sent beer and lead to Cromwell at Pembroke but that did not prevent the Protector from ordering the destruction of the castle, which was done in 1648, inefficiently fortunately, at a cost of £20. 4. 10, which impoverished the town. Haverfordwest had been incorporated in 1479, and in 1536, because of its central situation, it took the place of Pembroke as the county town. In 1543 it became a county in itself and, under the Act of Union, was allowed to return its own Member of Parliament; Richard Howell, merchant and mayor, was the first.

High-steepled St. Martin's, standing near the castle, is the oldest church but is much restored. St. Thomas's, with its tall thirteenth-century tower, contains the grave-slab of Richard the Palmer, bearing a floriated cross and a palm branch. St. Mary's, one of the finest churches in Wales, has a cathedral-like quality enhanced by the green light that falls across its spacious interior. The capitals of the Early English arcades are beautiful and amusing: a pig playing a crwth, an ape strumming a harp, a woman sticking out her tongue, and a miserable monk holding a tankard upside down. There are armorial memorials, a brass of 1651, and the mutilated effigy of a scallop-scripped pilgrim to Compostella. A pair of stalls, for the Mayor and Sheriff, has a fourteenth-century bench-end bearing the royal arms and a striking carving of St. Michael and the Dragon. The neglected ruin of the Augustinian Priory, down river, is a melancholy memorial to man's indifference. Haroldston House, the birthplace of Sir John Perrott, the town's greatest benefactor, is also ruinous. From Elizabethan times Haverfordwest was a busy port, trading mostly with the port of Bristol, as the quay-side inn, the Bristol Trader, reminds us, but with the coming of the South Wales Railway in 1853 the river traffic began to decline. The town has some fine Regency and early Victorian houses.

HUNDLETON (061006) has a modern brick church with a roof of red pantiles, built in 1933. Corston Beacon is surmounted by a round cairn in which a Beaker man was buried with a riveted knife-dagger by his side. A stone circle at Pennybridge was grubbed up by a farmer and its twelve stones were lined up against the hedge of the field. Orielton, now a field centre, was built in 1743 on a Norman site and was "haunted by unclean spirits" when Stephen Wyrriott lived there in 1188. It passed from that family, by marriage, to the Owens of Bodeon in Anglesey, who became the leading family in South Pembroke-shire.

LAWRENNY (017069) is a remote hamlet in the well-wooded Daugleddau sector of the National Park, beside the tall towered church of St. Caradog. The remains of the thirteenth-century house at Cresswell, known as The Palace, reveal a rectangular building with a turret at each corner; it may have been the home of Bishop Barlow of St. David's in the sixteenth century, but it was abandoned in favour of a site at Lawrenny which was rebuilt in the nineteenth century and demolished after the last war. Cresswell Chapel ruins stand nearby. Anthracite coal was exported from Cresswell Quay. Lawrenny Quay, at the confluence of the Cresswell and Carew rivers with the Cleddau, is approached by an open road edged with twisted oak trees. It is a pleasant holiday site and boating centre (Plate 35).

LITTLE HAVEN (857128), at the foot of a steep hill in a narrow valley, is a tiny, colourful seaside resort, gay with boats in summer. Little ships used to sail out with coal that was mined in pits nearby. On Strawberry Hill, above the village, an Iron Age fort has been recently excavated. The Point gives a sweeping view of St. Bride's Bay, from St. David's Head to Skomer Island.

LITTLE NEWCASTLE (980290) was one of a number of vills marking the northernmost intrusion of the Anglo-Normans; only the green mound of their castle remains. In this inland hamlet was born in 1682 one of the greatest of pirates, Bartholomew Roberts.

LLANGWM (084085) is a large village on the banks of the Cleddau, long renowned for its oysters and for its distinctiveness. The bellcoted church of St. Jerome is much restored: its fourteenth-century Roch chapel has canopied niche tombs with effigies of a knight and his lady, probably of the De la Roche family; a pillared piscina is decorated with plain shields. From Black Tar Point there are excellent views of the Cleddau, where Llangwm fishermen compass-net from their black tarred boats.

LLANRHIAN (819314). The church, half-hidden in a rookery, was rebuilt in 1836 and restored in 1891. Its unusual decagonal font carries the arms of Sir Rhys ap Thomas, which the family of neighbouring Rickeston bore. The coastward road leads to Porthgain (814327), a coastal hamlet scarred by derelict brickworks and quarrying remains, all abandoned in 1931. The once busy harbour (Plate 31) shelters a few small boats, and the Sloop Inn still holds the memory of an otherwise forgotten era. A path leads to Abereiddi (797312) where geese, cattle, and sheep graze down to the shingle and among the ruins of fishermen's cottages. A hollowed quarry to the right of the beach, known as the Blue Lagoon, makes a safe anchorage. The black cliffs contain *Didymograptus bifidus*, fossils like serrated hairpins found in the series of Ordovician rocks named after Llanfyrn, the farm above the bay. The isolated sandy beach of Traeth Llywn (798320), down a steep cliff path, may be approached along the coastal footpath from Abereiddi. Croesgoch (named the "red cross" after the blood that flowed along its four roads after a battle, it is said) has a yellow-fronted chapel built in 1859. Its Artramont Hotel was named after the Irish home of the Le Hunte family who once owned much land in the county.

LLANWNDA (933395) is named after St. Gwyndaf, to whom the early bellcoted church is dedicated. A boulder-strewn green gives a misleading impression of extensive megalithic remains, but there are three or more burial chambers in the parish and two standing stones. Garn Fawr is a fine hill-fort surrounded by hut-dwelling remains: from its 548-foot summit on a clear day may be seen Snowdonia and the Wicklow Hills, and on its western slope there is a small hut with a corbelled roof of the Irish "clochan" type. Evidence of early Christian settlement in the parish is provided by the remains of nine pillars inscribed with a cross, five of which have been built into the external walls of the church. A cliff-top chapel above Porth Sychan (909409) may have been an oratory built by St. Tegan to commemorate a safe landing. Trefaser (896379) is said to have been the birthplace of Asser, friend and adviser to King Alfred. Pwllderi (893385), where Atlantic grey seals haul out at most times of the year and feed their young in autumn, has been immortalised in a poem, written in the local dialect, by Dewi Emrys, the Welsh poet remembered on a wayside pillar above the bay. At Carreg Wastad (927406) a stone commemorates the last invasion of Britain, when the French landed here in 1797 and set up their headquarters at Trehowel Farm (*see* Fishguard). A French officer stole the chalice, inscribed LANVNDA, from the church and tried to sell it, saying it was from La Vendée!

LLAWHADEN (070174) is a corruption of Llanaidan, the church of St. Aidan (of Ferns). Its castle was built by Bishop Bernard in the twelfth century and it became the powerful residence of the Bishops of St. David's until the Dissolution. The present ruins date from the fourteenth century, considerably altered in the sixteenth. There are remains of the Priory of St. Mary, a hospice of wayfarers built by Bishop Beck in 1287. The church, standing by the river, has two towers. Llawhaden House is partly Tudor. Ridgeway House was given to John Foley, constable of Llawhaden Castle, by Bishop Adam Houghton in 1383. St. Kennox in 1620 was the home of Vicar Pritchard, author of *Cannwyll y Cymry* (the Candle of the Welsh), when he was Chancellor of St. David's and vicar of Llawhaden. The castle has been restored by the Ministry of Public Building and Works and is open daily.

LYDSTEP (087983) was largely built by the first Viscount St. David's, who erected a house for himself at Lydstep Haven, now a caravan site. In the village stand the ruins of the Palace of Arms, said to have been a hunting seat of Bishop Gower of St. David's, or else an armour house. Lydstep Head, National Trust property, has a car park, from which there are splendid views of Caldey and St. Margaret's Island, and a nature trail prepared by the West Wales Naturalists' Trust. Lydstep Caverns may be explored at low tide. On the submerged surface of Lydstep Bay was found the skeleton of a pig with a tree-trunk across its neck and, among its ribs, two flint arrowheads.

MANORBIER (066978) was described by Giraldus Cambrensis as "the paradise of all Wales". He was born here in 1146, of the family that gave Ireland its Barrys, Carews, Cogans, and Fitzgeralds, all sprung from Nest, "the Helen of Wales", and her husband, Gerald de Windsor. Giraldus travelled through Wales with Archbishop Baldwin of Canterbury in 1188 preaching the Third Crusade and wrote a diverting account of his tour in his *Itinerary through Wales*. His life's ambition to become Bishop of St. David's, so as to free the see from the yoke of Canterbury, was thwarted; he got no further than Archdeacon of Brecon. Manorbier Castle was built probably by Odo de Barri in the twelfth century; its impressive pile, viewed from the beach, is reminiscent of the great Crusader castles of Syria. The inner ward is approximately rectangular with a gate in the north-west face flanked by small round towers at each end. The church stands on the opposite slope of the valley; its nave is twelfth-century and its chancel, rebuilt in the fourteenth, contains an effigy of a member of the Barry family. The north transept has a window showing Master Richard, a monk, and Lady Margaret Tudor, together with the royal arms of William II. On Priest's Nose, the headland on the east of the bay, is the King's Quoit, a ruined cromlech.

MARLOES (785075), the most westerly village in south Pembrokeshire, has a grey bellcoted church containing a Norman font and a nineteenth-century baptistery sunk into the floor; there is a tradition that a former church, standing near the beach, was destroyed by the sea. The tall clock tower was built in honour of Lord Kensington (there is a Marloes Road in Kensington, W.8) by the people of the village, who have always derived their living from the sea (some as wreckers in the old days, it was said) and by gathering leeches for Harley Street in Marloes Mere. Early Iron Age men built the largest promontory fort in Pembrokeshire at the Deer Park; others established a settlement on Gateholm (goat island), which may be reached on foot at low tide. A narrow lane near the church leads to a National Park car park where you leave your car if you are prepared to walk half a mile to the long sandy beach of Marloes Sands. From Martin's Haven a boat leaves most summer days for Skomer, one of the finest bird islands in Britain and a national nature reserve administered by the West Wales Naturalists' Trust.

MILFORD HAVEN, a branched ria or drowned valley, stretching for 10 miles inland, contains "the finest port of Christendom". Its entrance and its upper reaches are in the National Park; between them is an area that has been devoted to industrial growth and which has quickly become a leading oil port. The leviathans of the deep bring in millions of tons of oil to feed four giant installations, together with one of the largest oil-fired power stations in Europe. The planning authorities have paid great regard to landscaping in the area of the development so as to minimise the impact of these huge projects which are essential in the national interest.

Aberdaugleddau (the estuary of the two Cleddau rivers) is the old name; here Arthur found the whelps of the she-wolf Rhymni during his hunt for the legendary boar, Twrch Trwyth, and here St. Brynach landed on his angel-guided mission to Nevern. Roman fleets must have found shelter here. Hubba the Dane is said to have wintered here at the time when the haven acquired its Norse name, Milford. Henry II, John, and other monarchs sailed from here to Ireland. Henry Tudor landed here to begin his march to Bosworth. Frobisher returned here from his second voyage to the Arctic; the pirate Callice could slink into the port while its admiral, Sir John Perrott, blinked to such an extent as to draw a rebuke from the Privy Council. The building of two blockhouses at the mouth of the Haven was begun in 1580, and in 1595 George Owen, lord of Cemais, advocated the siting of batteries at Dale Point and on Stack Rock and Thorn Island. But no coastal defences were built until the middle of the nineteenth century—the small forts at Dale Point, Stack Rock, Thorn Island, and West Blockhouse to defend the new dockyard at Pembroke Dock. Then Parliament ordered a second line of defence at South Hook and Chapel Bay, and a third line even, at Hubberston and Popton Point. Later a ring of forts was proposed to meet a landward attack on the dockyard, but only Scoveston Fort was completed. In 1790 Sir William Hamilton, who had inherited the land by marriage, obtained an Act of Parliament to build quays and docks, and to establish a market in the manor of Hubberston and Pill; and he left his nephew, Charles Greville, to set out a new port. Greville persuaded a colony of Quaker whalers from Nantucket, who earned their livelihood by providing spermaceti oil to light the lamps of London, to settle here. Soon afterwards the chequer-board town called Milford was built, and its streets commemorate the Quaker connexion in Starbuck Road and Nantucket Avenue. Greville invited Lord Nelson to visit Milford in 1802 and the great naval hero, accompanied by the Hamiltons, arrived in time to celebrate the fourth anniversary of the battle of the Nile. At a dinner held at Peter Cross's inn, known ever after as the Lord Nelson Hotel, Nelson proclaimed Milford, next to Trincomalee, the finest harbour he had ever seen.

MINWEAR Church (039130) adjoins Minwear Farm. It was given to the Commandery of the Knights of St. John of Jerusalem at Slebech, on the opposite side of the Eastern Cleddau, in about 1150. The road from Canaston Bridge (067152) to Minwear winds through a delightful part of the Slebech Forest. Stop at the National Park viewpoint, which has a free car park and picnic area. Leave your car and follow the forest walk, laid out for your benefit by the Forestry Commission, which is open from Easter to October; a descriptive leaflet, published by the Commission at 5p and available from information centres, will greatly enhance your enjoyment. Blackpool mill (Plate 30) was built by the Baroness de Rutzen in 1830, on a site once occupied by an iron-smelting works. It is now open as an agricultural museum and tea-rooms.

MOYLEGROVE (117447) was named after Matilda, the wife of Robert Martin, lord of Cemais (d. 1159). There was a small harbour at Ceibwr where little ships used to discharge their cargoes of culm and lime and where, it is said, a little bootlegging was carried on in ancient time. There are several remains of the Bronze Age and Iron Age to which numerous legends are attached. Castell Treruffydd (100448) was compared by George Owen to Tintagel. Nearby is a blowhole, the Witches' Cauldron, and a chalybeate well, Ffynnon Alwm, "inferior to none . . . but the Tunbridge Water". The Welsh name is *Trewyddel.*

NEVERN (083401) is one of the loveliest hamlets in Wales. Here was the stronghold of the Welsh ruler of the hundred of Cemais; the Norman invader Robert Fitz-Martin occupied it in about 1100, but his grandson William was driven out in 1191 by Lord Rhys, who probably built the second motte of this unique castle. The church (Plate 23) is dedicated to its founder, the Irish saint Brynach, and is Late Perpendicular. It is approached along a dark avenue of gnarled yew trees from one of which, the Bleeding Yew, there drips a blood-red sap. Beside the church porch stands a sixth-century stone pillar inscribed in Latin and in ogam to the memory of Vitalianus, a Welsh chieftain who had been given the Roman title of *emeritus.* A few steps away is the majestic Nevern Cross (Plate 22), standing 13 feet high and covered with interlaced and fretted panels, two of which bear unidentified inscriptions. Upon it, according to tradition, the cuckoo first sings on 7 April, which is St. Brynach's feast day. A window-sill in the church is another sixth-century pillar inscribed in ogam and in Latin to the memory of Maglocunus, son of Clutorius. There is a brass plate in the church to commemorate George Owen of Henllys, lord of Cemais (1552–1613), author of *The Description of Penbrokshire;* in the churchyard is the tomb of Tegid, the poet who assisted Lady Charlotte Guest in the translation into English of the early Welsh tales, *Y Mabinogi.* On a bare rock, above the church, a rough cross is cut in relief, perhaps a shrine on the pilgrim's route from St. Dogmael's to St. David's.

No parish has a greater number and variety of prehistoric remains. Pentre Ifan (099370) (Plate 16) is about the finest Neolithic burial chamber in Britain, and there are other cromlechs at Trellyffant (082425) and Llechydrybedd (101432). Crugiau Cemais (125416) is a cluster of Bronze Age barrows, adjoining which is a National Park viewpoint. There are three Iron Age camps at Penybenglog (119378). The southern

boundary of the parish is traversed by an ancient ridgeway
erroneously marked "Roman Road" on the Ordnance Survey
map, along which men travelled to and from Ireland in search
of copper and gold over 4,000 years ago.

NEWGALE (850220) has the longest beach in Pembrokeshire: over
two miles of firm, golden sand which once was forest. Giraldus
saw in 1172, and George Owen in 1600, the ebony-like stumps
of trees that are still exposed at very low tides after a storm.
The road that follows the shingle storm ridge is the prehistoric
"Welshman's Way". In 1690 the *Resolution* was blown ashore
and robbed "by the more unmerciful people of the neighbourhood". In 1882 the Duke of Edinburgh called and gave his
name to an inn that was to be washed away during a great
storm fourteen years later; when the landlady rescued her
daughter by hanging on to the stump of a tree and got away
with twenty sovereigns with which she opened the present inn,
on the landward side of the road. When the body of St.
Caradog was being carried through Newgale to St. David's
Cathedral for burial, "a prodigious fall of rain inundated the
whole country" but the silken pall "miraculously remained
dry and uninjured by the storm". The brook at Newgale forms
the western end of the "landsker", the linguistic divide
between the Welshery and the Englishery.

NEWPORT (057392) became the chief town of the ancient barony of
Cemais; it lies clustered below a Norman castle, but there
were earlier settlements on other sites. The earliest of these lies
immediately downstream of the bridge at Penybont where
Mesolithic men lived largely by fishing. The Welsh name
Trefdraeth indicates a settlement on the shore. New Stone Age
men buried their dead at Carreg Coetan cromlech nearby and
in the unique circle of cists at Cerrig y Gof (037389). An Iron
Age fort crowns the summit of Carn Ingli, the 1,138-foot crag
above the town. An early Christian cross-inscribed monument
stands before the thirteenth-century church tower. The church,
dedicated to St. Mary, was thoroughly restored in 1879. The
town grew around the castle established by William Martin,
lord of Cemais, when he moved his stronghold down the
estuary from Nevern. He granted the town a charter, some
time before 1215, conferring upon it the right to have a mayor
"in consultation with the lord". The castle was taken by
Llywelyn the Great in 1215 and by Llywelyn the Last in 1257,
and reduced by Owain Glyndwr in 1408. It was restored in
1859 and a residence built into the gateway. It is now a

guest-house and riding centre. A golf course adjoins Newport Sands.

NEYLAND (965051) was the site selected by Isambard Kingdom Brunel, in 1856, as the terminal of the South Wales Railway, and it became the port for the Irish steam packet until that service was transferred to Fishguard in 1906. Brunel's *Great Eastern* is commemorated in the name of a terrace in the town.

NOLTON HAVEN (860186) has a farm, a few cottages, a chapel, and a flat stretch of sand at low tide. A quay, now disappeared, was built in 1769 to export the coal and culm mined in the surrounding beds, and Nolton stone was used to make grindstones and mustard mills. The village of Nolton ("an old town"), a mile inland, has a bellcoted church containing the worn effigy of a knight, once used as a gatepost, and a carved stone bracket bearing three heads, one bearded. Druidston Haven has a beautiful, mile-long sandy beach.

PEMBROKE (919179) gave its name to the county palatine established in 1138, when Gilbert de Clare was made Earl of Pembroke; it is a corruption of the Welsh name *Penfro*, "land's end". It occupies a narrow ridge, upon which Arnulph de Montgomery built "a slender fortress of stakes and earth" in 1093. The present castle (Plate 27) was begun about 1190 by William Marshall, who built the great donjon. A vast limestone cavern, known as The Wogan, lies under the castle; narrow steps lead down to it from the northern hall and it has an exit to the river bank. In 1457 Henry Tudor was born at Pembroke Castle, and he spent most of his boyhood here. During the Civil Wars the castle was held for Parliament by the mayor, John Poyer, who later declared for the King; Cromwell himself came to lay siege to it, a siege that lasted 48 days. Poyer was shot at Covent Garden and the castle was dismantled by Cromwell's command. Parts of the town wall, which had three gates, remain. St. Mary's Church, near the castle, was built in the thirteenth century, and has stone monuments from the early seventeenth century onwards. Monkton Priory was originally a cell of the Abbey of Séez in Normandy; its remains, including a dovecote, are partly incorporated in Priory Farm; the choir and sanctuary became the chancel of the parish church of Monkton which was restored in 1887. The church has several monuments to the Owens of Orielton (now a field centre) and the Meyricks of Bush (now a grammar school).

PEMBROKE DOCK (966034) was established at Paterchurch (or Patrick Church) when the Admiralty transferred the Royal dockyard from Milford Haven in 1814. The first ships, *Valorous* and *Ariadne*, were launched two years later. The town was built on a gridiron plan with wide streets. The dockyard was closed in 1926 but it was used as a Sunderland base by the Royal Air Force during the last war. It is now a popular yachting centre.

PENALLY (118991), a corruption of the Welsh name *Penalun*, is believed to be the birthplace of St. Teilo and here, we are told, "were the tombs of his father and where his patrimony lay". Excavations at Longbury Bank Cave produced fragments of imported pottery, including amphorae and red bowls, and human remains which suggest that the cave was the retreat of a hermit. It may be that the site of the important monastery known to have existed at Penally was in this vicinity. The parish church, dedicated to St. Teilo, has a decorated slab-cross and three broken shafts of the tenth and eleventh centuries; the motifs they bear are of Saxon derivation and indicate the close connexion between Wessex and West Wales. Tenby golf course adjoins the village. The road from Penally to Pembroke follows the ancient ridgeway and retains that name.

PRESELY. Stretching across North Pembrokeshire is a range of smooth, rounded hills, covered in heather and gorse and scattered with boulders and sheep. They are the Presely Hills (Plates 14 and 15). "Presely as a whole", said Jacquetta Hawkes, "is of far greater interest in our prehistory than any single monument." Neolithic burial chambers are found on its slopes. An ancient trackway, illogically called the Flemings' Way, along the ridge of the hills was used as a prehistoric trade route, when axes of preselite (igneous rock from Presely) were traded in Ireland and Bronze Age men brought back copper and gold. (Pembrokeshire folklore tells of sea traders with pieces of gold landing at St. David's Head.) From Carn Menyn (143326) and Carn Alw, 83 bluestones—pillars of ophitic dolerite weighing up to 4 tons each—were transported to Stonehenge in about 1700 B.C. "One of the most dramatic events in our prehistory", affirms Mrs. Hawkes, "and perhaps the most weighty proof of the power of religious sanctions in prehistoric Europe." The only stone circle in the county may be seen on the open moorland at Gors Fawr (134294). Moel Drygarn (157336) is topped by a splendid univallate Iron Age hill-fort (Plate 18). King Arthur and his knights hunted the legendary boar, Twrch Trwyth, across the slopes of Presely, according to early Welsh tales. Foel Cwmcerwyn, at 1,760 feet, is the highest point of the range; between it and Foel Eryr (1,533 feet), at Bwlchgwynt, the old Cardigan-Haverfordwest road (B 4329) crosses the Flemings' Way at a height of 1,328 feet. From here, on a clear day, Snowdonia can be seen, and the Wicklow Hills to the west and Dunkery Beacon across the Bristol Channel.

RAMSEY ISLAND (705240) is privately owned and managed as a nature reserve by the Royal Society for the Protection of Birds. Its beaches are the favourite breeding grounds of the Atlantic grey seal. Boats leave from Porth Stinan (St. Justinian's).

ROCH (881212) is a small village beneath a castle-crested igneous outcrop. The castle is a pele-tower of the thirteenth century, said to have been built on a crag by Adam de la Roche to defy a prophecy that he would die by the bite of a serpent, but the venomous viper was carried into the castle in a bundle of faggots and Adam perished. In 1601 the castle was purchased by a neighbouring squire, William Walter, whose great-grand-daughter, Lucy Walter, was mistress to Charles II and mother of the ill-fated Duke of Monmouth. The castle was converted into a private residence in 1902 by the first Viscount St. David's. The parish church, which stands within a raised circular churchyard, is modern except for the porch.

ROSEBUSH (074293) was developed as a mountain holiday resort by John Babington Macaulay, a nephew of Lord Macaulay, in the 1870s. He laid out gardens and planted them with trees and shrubs, excavated lakes which he stocked with goldfish, and built a small hotel of corrugated iron zinc. A railway was laid from Clunderwen in 1876, and another from Fishguard three years later, to bring the masses to Rosebush and to carry slates from its quarry. But no one came and the quarries are but a scar on the pale green velvet slopes.

ST. BRIDE'S (803109). A church, a rectory, and a cottage in a red stone cove, like the great bay they face, bear the name of St. Brigid of Kildare, whose cult is as widespread as the Irish colonisation of the sixth century. An earlier chapel was washed away by the sea and traces of stone-lined graves are visible near the old lime kiln. The church was restored in 1860 except for the steps and doorway to the rood loft. The mansion to the west of the church, built about 1800, is now a hospital named after Lord Kensington who once owned St. Bride's.

9A

ST. DAVID'S (753252)—*Tŷ Ddewi*, the house of David—is the smallest city in Britain. It stands above the valley in which the patron saint of Wales, Dewi the son of Sant, built his monastery in the sixth century, out of the sight of marauding sea-rovers. But this did not prevent the Norsemen from attacking it no fewer than ten times. The present cathedral (Plate 24) was begun by the Norman bishop Peter de Leia about 1182. Bishop Gower built the magnificent stone choir screen and the Bishop's Palace during the first half of the fourteenth century. In the fifteenth century, the "boldly and joyously irreverent" misereres were carved in the choir stalls, one of which is set apart for the reigning sovereign and was occupied for the first time by Her Majesty the Queen on 7 August 1955. The elaborately carved nave roof of grey Irish oak, with pendants "of almost Arabian gorgeousness", and the fan-vaulted ceiling of the Holy Trinity chapel, are of the sixteenth century. In 1793 John Nash unsuccessfully rebuilt the west front, and seventy years later Sir Gilbert Scott was commissioned to carry out a major restoration. The shrine of St. David was built in 1275 on the north side of the presbytery but the relics of the saint are in a movable shrine behind the High Altar. In the centre of the presbytery stands the tomb of Edmund Tudor, Earl of Richmond, father of Henry VII, whose body was brought from the Grey Friars at Carmarthen when his grandson dissolved the monasteries. Effigies represent the great Lord Rhys, last prince of South Wales, and members of his family, various priests, bishops, knights, and Giraldus Cambrensis, and there are early Christian monuments from the fifth century onward; one commemorates Hedd and Isaac, sons of Bishop Abraham who was killed by the Norse in 1080.

ST. DAVID'S PENINSULA is a bare, windswept plateau dotted with substantially built farm settlements. From it rise rugged monadnocks and around it there are several creeks and bays. Caerfai is approached by a cliff path and has a sandy beach. St. Non's contains the ruin of a chapel, a well dedicated to the patron saint's mother and a house, and a chapel converted by the Passionist Fathers. Porth Clais was the harbour of the monastic community of David and here the legendary wild boar, Twrch Trwyth, landed from Ireland; here too, tradition says, David was baptised. Porth Stinan has the ruins of St. Justinian's chapel and a lifeboat station; boats cross to Ramsey and make trips around the island. From Porth Mawr, or Whitesand Bay, St. Patrick is said to have sailed to Ireland;

his chapel is marked by a plaque near the beach. It has a wide stretch of sand and a large car park. A cliff path leads to another sandy beach at Porth Melgan and on to Penmaen Dewi (St. David's Head) where there is a fine Iron Age promontory fort. The modest climb to the top of Carn Llidi (595 feet) is rewarding; Snowdonia and the Wicklow Hills may be seen on clear days. Clegyr Boia is crowned by an Iron Age camp built on a much earlier Neolithic settlement. Seals breed around the coast and especially on Ramsey, and choughs and peregrine falcons may be sighted.

ST. DOGMAEL'S (165460), or *Llandudoch*, is an old fishing village on the estuary of the Teifi. Robert Fitz-Martin, lord of Cemais, established an abbey here early in the twelfth century on the site of an old monastery; its remains have been well preserved by the Ministry of Public Building and Works (H.M.S.O. official guide-book). The parish church, dedicated to St. Thomas the Martyr, was built in 1847 in the grounds of the abbey. An early Christian monument, inscribed in Latin and in ogam, to the memory of Sagranus, son of Cunotamus, provided the key to the ogam alphabet in 1848. A road along the Teifi leads to Poppit Sands which has a large caravan park and an extensive sandy beach.

ST. MARGARET'S ISLAND (120793) is a nature reserve managed by the West Wales Naturalists' Trust; landing is by permit only.

SAUNDERSFOOT (135045) is an attractive seaside resort with a sandy beach and a small sheltered harbour, which was built in 1829 for the export of the anthracite coal mined in the locality. The tree-capped cliffs expose the folding and faulting of the Coal Measures; an anticline on the beach (Plate 4) is a geological monument. The parish church, dedicated to St. Issel (the Welsh saint Usullt), lies in a lovely wooded hollow, a remnant of the vast and ancient forest of Coedrath. It has a fine embattled Norman tower and a fourteenth-century font.

SKOKHOLM (735050), composed of Old Red Sandstone, has been described by R. M. Lockley in several of his earlier books. He farmed the island from 1927 to 1939 and established there the first bird observatory in Britain.

SKOMER (725094) is a mass of grey igneous rock, in contrast to Skokholm. Its original Norse name was *Scalmey*, indicating the cloven shape of the island. There are remains of hut-circles and enclosures of the Iron Age, and the island was farmed until 1958 when it was bought jointly by the West Wales Naturalists' Trust and the Nature Conservancy and established as a national nature reserve. It is one of the finest seabird islands in Britain, and a riot of wild flowers in the spring and early summer. It is open to visitors, boats crossing daily from Martin's Haven during the summer.

SOLVA (805245) lies in a ria, or drowned valley, on the northern shore of St. Bride's Bay. Lower Solva, gay with colour-washed cottages, was built around the little harbour, just out of sight of sea marauders. Here, in 1773, the wooden structure of the first lighthouse to be placed on the Smalls was assembled. A quantity of flint implements has been found around Upper Solva. Across the inlet is the Gribin, a ridged headland with an Iron Age fort. Middle Mill, along a narrow, steep-sided valley, has a large quarry and a small woollen factory. The parish church was built at Whitchurch in 1877.

STACKPOLE (984964) is a small village that was built to serve Stackpole Court, the home of the Earls Cawdor, now demolished. The church, at Stackpole Elidyr or Cheriton, nearly a mile away, has fourteenth-century effigies of Richard de Stackpole and his wife, and a seventeenth-century monument of Roger Lort and his wife and their twelve children, among others. Stackpole Quay is a cove carved out of a quarry, with a stone jetty, from which a footpath leads over the cliff-tops to Barafundle Bay, a quiet sandy cove.

TENBY (132004) takes its name from *Dinbych-y-Pysgod*—"the little fort of the fishes"—and it appears in one of the earliest recorded Welsh poems, which an unknown poet wrote in the ninth century in praise of "the fine fortress that stood over the sea". The fragmentary remains on Castle Hill are of the thirteenth century. The town was sacked by Maelgwn, son of Lord Rhys, in 1187, and again by Llywelyn the Last in 1260. It was granted a charter in 1402 but incorporation was not achieved until 1581. The Tudor Merchant's House (Plate 29), now a museum, and Plantagenet House are of the fifteenth century. During the Civil Wars, Tenby was garrisoned and besieged by both sides. Parliamentary ships engaged land batteries in 1643; some of the cannon serve as bollards around the harbour. From the middle of the eighteenth century the town became popular as a health resort and new houses were built to accommodate the visiting gentry. In 1811 sea-water baths were built at Laston House (with an appropriate quotation from Euripides over the door) by Sir William Paxton, together with a reservoir and a piped water supply. Much of Georgian Tenby is caught in the works of Charles

Norris, who is said to have been attracted to the town by the praises of Walter Savage Landor. St. Mary's is the largest parish church in Wales and dates from the thirteenth century, but there was an earlier church. It contains the tomb of Robert Recorde, the mathematician and inventor of the sign of equality. It has an elegant arcade and a fine fifteenth-century wagon roof over the chancel and sanctuary. St. Julian's is a small fisherman's chapel beside the harbour. The town walls have round towers at intervals, and the barbican in front of the south gate has five arches. Tenby Museum is on Castle Hill. St. Catherine's Island's nineteenth-century fort is now a zoo.

TREFIN (840325) is a cruciform coastal village, the home of countless "Cape-Horners" and the birthplace of the former Archdruid Trefin. The *Black Book of St. David's* states, in 1326, that a fair was held in the village on the feast of St. Martin, and on that day the women made traditional mutton pies called *pasteiod Ffair Fartin*. Bishop David Martin built an episcopal palace in the village but there is hardly a trace of it now. At Aberfelin nearby is the ruin of the mill that inspired the poet Crwys to write his famous poem *Melin Trefin*.

VELINDRE FARCHOG (100390)—"Knight's Milton"—was named after a mill which has lately disappeared. A small Elizabethan house with mullioned windows, called The College, was built by George Owen, lord of Cemais, for use as a school.

WISTON (023182) was founded by Wizo the Fleming in the twelfth century. The castle was taken by the Welsh in 1147 and again in 1193 and was destroyed by Llywelyn the Great in 1220. The motte, with its bean-shaped bailey, is crowned by the only shell-keep in the county. On Colby Moor, on 1 August 1645, the Royalists were battered by the Parliamentary forces to such an extent that a "Colby Moor rout" has become a proverbial expression in Pembrokeshire.

APPENDICES

I. Welsh Place-Names

Welsh place-names predominate in the north of the county while many survive in the English area of the south, though often in a form that is no longer recognisable. Cosheston is universally accepted as the English name of a typical Anglo-Norman village, but its name derives from a Welsh princeling, Cystennin ab Erbin. His brother, Cybi ab Erbin, gave his name to the equally English-sounding Gupton. Others are less heavily disguised: Trefloyne is a justifiable anglicisation of Trellwyn, as Crunwere is of Cronwern. Some remain pure, or near pure, in form: Pwllcrochan, Llangwm, Llanstadwell, Begelly, Kilgetty, Redberth, Narberth.

Likewise, in the Welshery, there are places which have original English names, like the small Norman garrison town of Newport, the manors of Moylegrove and Monington, and the vills that mark the northernmost flow of the Anglo-Normans: Little Newcastle, New Moat, Henry's Moat.

Welsh place-names are descriptive of the location (*Dan-y-deri* = under the oak trees) and of the physical features (*Carnlwyd* = grey cairn; *Blaenafon* = source of a river; *Cnwcau* = knolls). They often bear the names of animals or birds (*Ogof cadno* = fox's cave; *Carreg y Wylan* = seagull's rock) and of trees and plants (*Cwmonnen* = ash vale; *Llain banadl* = broom strip). Many are named after people (*Bedd Bys Samson* = grave of Samson's finger; *Carn Ingli* = Ingli's cairn; *Fagwyr Einion* = Eynon's wall), in addition to the many saints' names that follow *llan* or *eglwys* (church), such as *Llaneilfyw* (St. Elvis' church) and *Eglwyswrw* (the church of St. Wrw).

Pronunciation. Welsh pronunciation is robust and phonetic. Any attempt to pronounce a Welsh place-name in a mincing manner not only makes it unrecognisable to the local people but also causes offence. People who take trouble to enunciate *Ashby-de-la-Zouch* or *Colombey-les-Deux-Eglises* should not be content to pronounce Mynydd Bach as "money back" or Gelliwastad as "jelly wasted". Welsh names sound much better when spoken properly and the following notes on consonantal and vowel sounds are intended to be of guidance:

b, d, h, l, m, n, p, t, have the same sound as in English;
c is always hard as in *cat*;
ch as in *loch*;
dd as in *thine*;
f is like *v*;
ff is like *f* in *fish*;
g is hard as in *go*;
r is trilled as in *merry*;
s is hard as in *essay*;
ll is produced by putting your tongue against the roof of your mouth
and hissing like a gander.

The following double letters have distinctive sounds:
ng as in *long*, or sometimes *longer* (*e.g. Bangor*);
ph as in *pheasant*;
rh as in *rhino*;
th as in *think*.

The Welsh vowels are *a, e, i, o, u, w,* and *y*: it should always be
remembered that *w* and *y* are also vowels in Welsh. Each vowel has
two values, long and short. They are short when followed by *c, m,
ng, p, t,* or by two or more consonants, and they are long when
followed by *b, ch, d, f, ff, g, s,* or *th:*

	Long		Short
a	as in *barn*;		as in *ban*;
e	as in *pane*;		as in *pen*;
i	as in *eel*;		as in *ill*;
o	as in *dole*;		as in *doll*;
u	as in *keel*;		as in *kill*;
w	as in *pool*;		as in *pull*;
y	as in *fur*,		as in *fun*,
	or as in *dean*.		or as in *din*.

Mutation. The mutation of initial consonants presents problems for
the uninitiated, especially when searching for a word in a dictionary.
The consonants *p, t, c, b, d, g, m, ll,* and *rh* soften to *b, d, g, f, dd*
(*g* disappears), *f, l, r* respectively in certain circumstances such as:

(*a*) when a noun follows the preposition *ar* (upon), *e.g.*
   ar+perth-Arberth;
(*b*) when a female noun follows the definite article, *e.g.*
   y+pont-y Bont,
   y+cath-y Gath,
   dan+y+derwen-Danydderwen;

(*c*) when an adjective follows a feminine noun, *e.g.*
croes+coch-Croesgoch,
ffynnon+glas-Ffynnon-las;

(*d*) when the genitive follows a feminine noun, *e.g.*
carn+merched-Carn Ferched,
tref+traeth-Trefdraeth,
llan+gwern-Llanwern;

(*e*) when a personal name in the genitive follows a masculine noun,
e.g.
llan+fihangel-Llanfihangel,
tŷ+Dewi-Tŷddewi;

(*f*) when a noun or adjective is the second element in a compound,
e.g.
sych+pant-Sychbant,
bwch+tŷ-Bwchdŷ,
gwyn+bryn-Gwynfryn,
brith+tir-Brithdir;

(*g*) when a noun follows an adjective (except for *ll* and *th*), *e.g.*
hen+tref-Hendref,
hen+llan-Henllan.

Stress. The accent is usually on the penultimate syllable. Where it is
on the last syllable this is normally indicated by the use of a hyphen,
e.g. Efail-wen, but some names are so well known that it is not
considered necessary to insert a hyphen, *e.g. Abergwaun*.

Spelling. The spelling of place-names in this book follows the
principles laid down in *A Gazetteer of Welsh Place-Names* (ed.
Elwyn Davies, 1958) by the language and literature committee of the
Board of Celtic Studies of the University of Wales. It does not follow
the spelling forms given by the Ordnance Survey, which are
notoriously incorrect, although efforts are now being made to correct
them.

II. Scheduled Ancient Monuments

BURIAL MOUNDS AND MEGALITHIC MONUMENTS

	Grid Reference
Ambleston, Parc-y-llyn burial chamber	SM 982265
Angle, Devil's Quoit burial chamber	SM 886008
Bayvil, Crugiau Cemais	SN 125414 to 126417
Bayvil, cup-marked stone 370 yards E of Tre-foel	SN 102403
Bayvil, Pant-y-groes round barrow	SN 109422
Boulston, Hanton round barrows	SM 985144
Burton burial chamber	SM 972082
Camrose, Plumstone Mountain round barrow	SM 913235
Camrose, Plumstone Rock round barrows	SM 972082
Carew, round barrow N of Rosemary Lane	SN 043058
Carew, round barrow S of Rosemary Lane	SN 042054
Carew and Manorbier, Carew Beacon round barrows	SN 041008 to 042007
Castellan, round barrow on W slope of Freni Fawr	SN 199351
* Castlemartin, Brownslade round barrow	SR 905972
* Castlemartin, Mount Sion Down round barrow	SR 917953
Clydau, Castell Blaidd round barrow	SN 241308
Clydau, Crug Bach round barrow	SN 251323
Clydau and Penrhydd, Freni Fach round barrow	SN 226348
Dinas standing stone	SN 008388
Fishguard South, Tymeini standing stone	SM 996377
Haroldston West, Harold stone	SM 861147
Haroldston West, Lamber round barrow	SM 894148
Haroldston West, standing stones near Upper Lodge	SM 861142
Hayscastle, Rhindaston-fawr standing stone	SM 896244
Hayscastle Tump round barrow	SM 902246
Henry's Moat, Budloy standing stone	SN 065285
Henry's Moat, Dyffryn stone circle	SN 059284
Hubberston, Long Stone burial chamber	SM 892071
Hundleton, Corston Beacon round barrow	SR 933999
Hundleton, Dry Burrows round barrows	SR 948997
Jordanston Hill round barrow	SM 922331
Lampeter Velfrey, Llan burial chamber	SN 147140
Lampeter Velfrey, Llanmarlais round barrow	SN 178163
Letterston, Pendre round barrow	SM 948298
Little Newcastle, Colston burial chamber	SM 982282
Llandeilo, Foel Cwmcerwyn round cairns	SN 095315 to 094311
Llandeloy, Treffynnon burial chamber	SM 854286
Llanfihangel Penbedw and Penrhydd, round barrows on summit of Freni Fawr	SN 202349
Llanfyrnach, round barrow 300 yards SW of Crymych	SN 182338
Llangolman, Gate standing stone	SN 111303
Llanhywel, Lecha burial chamber	SM 812271

	Grid Reference
Llanhywel, White House burial chamber	SM 826283
Llanllawer, Parc y Meirw standing stones	SM 998359
Llanrhian, Bickney round barrow	SM 831314
Llanwnda, Carn Wnda burial chamber	SM 933392
Llanwnda, Garn Gilfach burial chamber	SM 908390
Llanwnda, Garn Wen burial chambers	SM 947390
Llanwnda, Pen-rhiw burial chamber	SM 943391
Llanycefn, Rhiwiau round barrow	SN 096229
Llanychaer, Mynydd Cilciffeth round barrows	SN 009324
Llanychwydog, Clun-gath round barrow	SN 016366
Llawhaden, Dan-y-coed circle	SN 078188
Llawhaden, Gelli earthwork	SN 079197
Ludchurch and Lampeter Velfrey, New House round barrows	SN 157113 to 160114
Maenclochog, Cnwc round cairns	SN 088304 and 086302
Maenclochog, Cornel-bach standing stones	SN 082279
Maenclochog, Eithbed burial chambers	SN 081286
Maenclochog, Galchen-fach standing stone	SN 087279
Manorbier, Bier Hill round barrows	SN 070001
Manorbier, King's Quoit burial chamber	SS 059973
Mathry, Carreg Samson burial chamber	SM 848335
Mathry, Penlanmabws-uchaf burial chamber	SM 890307
Mathry, Trewalter Llwyd burial chamber	SM 868317
Mathry, Tynewydd-grug standing stone	SM 925287
Meline, Beddyrafanc burial chamber	SN 108346
Mynachlog-ddu, Gors Fawr stone circle	SN 135294
Mynachlog-ddu, Mountain burial chamber	SN 166328
Mynachlog-ddu, Tynewydd standing stones	SN 118310
Mynachlog-ddu, Waun Lwyd standing stones	SN 157313
Narberth North, Redstone Cross round barrows	SN 110164
Nevern, Foel Eryr round cairn	SN 066321
Nevern, Foel Feddau round cairn	SN 102323
Nevern, Llechydrybedd burial chamber	SN 101432
Nevern, Panparce standing stone	SN 090354
Nevern, Parc-lan standing stones	SN 090357
† Nevern, Pentre Ifan burial chamber	SN 099370
Nevern, Tafarn-bwlch standing stone	SN 081339
Nevern, Tre-fach standing stone	SN 064350
Nevern, Trellyffant burial chamber	SN 082425
Nevern, Waun Mawn standing stones	SN 080339 to 084341
Newport, Carn Ffoi round barrows	SN 047378
Newport, Carn Ingli round barrows	SN 065380
Newport, Carreg Goetan burial chamber	SN 061394
Newport, Cerrig y Gof burial chamber	SN 037389
Pembroke, Kingston burial chamber	SR 992993
Pembroke, Rose Valley round barrow	SM 997006
Penrhydd, Rhos Goch round barrow	SN 197340
Penrhydd, round barrow on E slope of Freni Fawr	SN 206347
Puncheston, Fagwr-fran standing stone	SN 004316
Puncheston, Marsh round barrow	SN 006309

	Grid Reference
Pwllcrochan, Wallaston round barrows	SM 925003
Rudbaxton, round barrow 180 yards N of Ramswood House	SM 987208
St. David's, Carn Llidi burial chambers	SM 736279
St. David's, Coetan Arthur burial chamber	SM 725281
St. David's, Maen Sigl burial chamber	SM 733277
St. Dogmael's, Foxhill round barrow	SN 151453
St. Dogmaels, Pant-y-groes crugiau	SN 141456 to 142457
St. Dogwell's, Garn Turne burial chamber, etc.	SM 979273
St. Dogwell's, Lower Broadmoor standing stone	SM 952277
St. Edren's, Clun-ffwrn burial chamber	SM 898289
St. Edren's, Tre-hale standing stone	SM 888297
St. Edren's, Trehywel burial chamber	SM 893289
St. Elvis burial chamber	SM 812239
St. Ishmael's, standing stone 320 yards S of Mabesgate	SM 827076
St. Ishmael's, standing stone NNW of Sandy Haven	SM 848083
St. Nicholas, Ffynnondridian standing stone	SM 921365
St. Nicholas, Garn-llys burial chamber	SM 906349
St. Nicholas, Rhos y Clegyrn circle and standing stone	SM 913355
St. Petrox, Sampson Cross standing stone	SR 962963
St. Petrox, Stackpole Farm standing stone	SR 968959
St. Twynnells, Love Stone, Loveston	SR 948968
Stackpole Elidyr, Stackpole Warren standing stone	SR 983951
Uzmaston, Good Hook round barrow	SM 987166
Uzmaston, round barrow	SM 970148
Walton West, Woodland round barrow	SM 859117
Whitchurch, Tremaenhir standing stones	SM 827263

CAMPS AND ANCIENT SETTLEMENTS

Angle, West Pickard camp	SM 862010
Bayvil, Cwm-gloyn camp	SN 104398
* Bosherston, Buckspool Down camp	SM 955934
Bosherston, Fishponds camp	SM 971949
Brawdy, Castle Villa camp	SM 881277
Camrose, Crowhill rath	SM 950173
Camrose, Plumstone rath	SM 922232
Carew, Park camp	SN 063048
Castlebythe, Castell-y-fuwch	SN 024291
Castlebythe, Wern camp	SN 018302
* Castlemartin, Bulliber camp (East)	SM 907965
* Castlemartin, Bulliber Hill camp	SM 902966
* Castlemartin, Flimston Bay camp	SM 930945
Castlemartin, King's Mill camp	SM 924987
* Castlemartin, Linney Head camp	SM 888957
Dale, Dale Point promontory fort	SM 824052
Dale, Great Castle Head rath	SM 798056
Fishguard South, Cronllwyn earthwork	SM 986353

	Grid Reference
Haroldston West, Black Point rath	SM 859153
Hayscastle, Ford camp	SM 948265
Hayscastle, West Ford camp	SM 947256
Herbrandston, South Hook camp	SM 866063
Hundleton, Bowett Wood camp	SM 972007
Jordanston, Castell Hendre-wen	SM 921337
Lampeter Velfrey, Blaengwaithnoe camp	SN 151123
Little Newcastle, Summerton camp	SM 990301
Llanddewi Velfrey, Caerau Gaer	SN 139161
Llanddewi Velfrey, Llanddewi Gaer	SN 145160
Llandysilio West, Castell-gwyn	SN 110217
Llanfair Nant-y-gof, Bucket camp	SM 950310
Llanfair Nant-y-gof, Castell Cwmwyntyll	SM 964311
Llanfair Nant-y-gof, Wauncastell camp	SM 971323
Llanfyrnach, gaer 300 yards W of Glandwr Farm	SN 186283
Llangolman, Pencraig-mawr camp	SN 118263
Llanrhian, Castell Coch	SM 840338
Llanstinan, Caer Penbicas	SM 959327
Llanstinan, Castell Pant-y-Philip	SM 952335
Llantood, Castell Felinganol	SN 164422
Llanwnda, Castell Cledyff	SM 920398
Llanwnda, Dinas-mawr camp	SM 887387
Llanwnda, Garn Fawr camp	SM 895388
Llanwnda, Garn Fechan camp	SM 901389
Llanychlwydog, Castell Pengegin	SN 039344
Llanychlwydog, huts on Mynydd Melyn	SN 027362
Llawhaden, camp 400 yards SE of Drim	SN 067193
Llawhaden, camp ½ mile SW of Gelly Bridge	SN 078189
Llawhaden, camp ¼ mile NW of Holgan	SN 073182
Llawhaden, camp 220 yards NE of Stoney-ford	SN 070183
Llawhaden, camp 400 yards NE of Stoney-ford	SN 071184
Llawhaden, Drim camp	SN 064197
Llawhaden, Faenor Gaer	SN 094171
Ludchurch, Castell Meherin camps	SN 147117
Ludchurch, Longstone camp	SN 149099
Marloes, Deer Park promontory fort	SM 758090
Marloes, hut-groups on Gateholm Island	SM 770072
Marloes, hut-groups, cairns, and cliff castle on Skomer Island	SM 725094
Marloes, Watery Bay rath	SM 768079
Mathry, Ynysycastell	SM 851339
Meline, Carn Alw hill-fort	SN 138337
Meline, Castell-llwyd	SN 113376
Meline, Castell-mawr	SN 118378
Meline, Cwm Penybenglog camp	SN 118372
Milford, Priory rath	SM 905071
Monington, Glan-dwr-isaf camp	SN 126447
Moylegrove, Castell Treruffydd	SN 100448
Narberth South, Molleston camp	SN 087130
Nevern, Banc Llywdlos hut-group	SN 093331
Nevern, Castell Henllys	SN 118390

	Grid Reference
Nevern, Foel Eryr hut-group	SN 067320
Nevern, Tre-fach camp	SN 087408
Nevern, Tre-gynon camp	SN 052346
Nevern, Waun Clun-coch hut-group	SN 106313
New Moat, Rhyd-brown camp	SN 067223
Newport, Carn Ffoi camp	SN 048379
Newport, Carn Ingli camp	SN 062372
Newport, Carn Ingli Common hut-circles	SN 055368
Newport, Mynydd Caregog hut-circle	SN 043365
Pwllcrochan, West Pennar camp	SM 933030
Pwllcrochan, West Popton camp	SM 907038
Robeston Wathen, Bush Inn camp	SN 076155
Robeston West, Rickeston rath	SM 870095
Roch, Slade camp	SM 892226
Rosemarket rath	SM 953080
Rudbaxton rath	SM 985188
St. Bride's, Tower Point rath	SM 790108
St. David's, Caerfai camp	SM 763240
St. David's, Castell Heinif	SM 724247
St. David's, Clegyrfwya camp	SM 737251
St. David's, hut-circles and ancient enclosures NW of Carn Llidi	SM 732283
St. David's Head camp	SM 722279
St. Dogmael's, Caerau	SN 124454
St. Dogmael's, Pencastell promontory fort	SN 110459
St. Dogwell's, Hazel Grove camp (North)	SM 964236
St. Dogwell's, Hazel Grove camp (South)	SM 965235
St. Dogwell's, Little Treffgarne camp	SM 961248
St. Dogwell's, Little Treffgarne Wood camp	SM 961245
St. Dogwell's, Sealyham Quarries camp	SM 959275
St. Dogwell's, Sealyham Rocks camp	SM 969283
Slebech, Castle Lake camp	SN 021129
Slebech, Picton Point camp	SN 002118
Stackpole Elidyr, Greenala camp	SM 007966
Stackpole Elidyr, Stackpole earthwork	SR 987966
Steynton, Denant rath	SM 922130
Steynton, Thornton rath	SM 905079
Talbenny, Howney Stone rath	SM 820128
Talbenny, Mill Haven rath	SM 816125
Treffgarne, Great Treffgarne Rocks camp	SM 956250
Treffgarne, Great Treffgarne Wood camp	SM 960233
Vorlan, Castell Vorlan	SN 091266
Walton East, Scollock rath	SN 019242
Walton East, Walton rath	SN 022231
Walton West and Walwyn's Castle, Woodland rath	SM 854118
Walwyn's Castle, Capeston rath	SM 868096
Walwyn's Castle, rath S of St. James's Church	SM 873110
Walwyn's Castle, Roman's Castle	SM 895106
Walwyn's Castle, Syke rath	SM 871103
* Warren, Crocksydam camp	SR 935943

	Grid Reference
Warren, Merrion camp	SR 940975
Whitchurch, Porth-y-rhaw camp	SM 787242
Whitechurch, Moel Drygarn camp	SN 157336
Wiston, Lamborough camp	SN 027198
Wiston, Woodbarn camp	SN 017170

ROMAN REMAINS

Ambleston, Castle Flemish	SN 007267

CROSSES AND INSCRIBED STONES

Bridell, inscribed pillar-stone in churchyard	SN 177421
Capel Colman, Maen Colman	SN 216383
† Carew Cross	SN 046036
Cilgerran, inscribed stone in churchyard	SN 190431
Jordanston, inscribed stone at Llangwarren Farm	SM 929313
Llandeilo, inscribed stones outside ruined church of St. Teilo[1]	SN 099269
Llanfyrnach, inscribed stone near Glandŵr Independent Chapel	SN 191286
Llanfyrnach, Rhyd-y-gath pillar-cross	SM 215313
Llangan West, St. Canna's Chair	SN 177188
Llanllawer, two pillar-crosses in churchyard	SM 987359
Llanrhian, Mesur y Dorth cross-incised stone	SM 839306
Llanwnda, incised cross at cemetery cross-roads	SM 937359
Llanwnda, Llanwnnwr cross-slab	SM 895405
Llanychaer, pillar-cross in churchyard	SM 992345
Llanychlwydog, four pillar-crosses in churchyard	SN 012345
Llys-y-frân, Velindre pillar-cross	SN 044258

[1] Removed into Maenclochog Church

Mathry, two pre-Norman gravestones in churchyard	SM 879320
Morvil, pillar-cross in churchyard	SN 037307
Nevern, High Cross in churchyard	SN 083400
Nevern, inscribed stone in churchyard	SN 083400
Nevern, rock-hewn cross 250 yards W of church	SN 081400
Nevern, Tre-bwlch pillar-crosses	SN 086352
Newport, pillar-cross in churchyard	SN 057389
Newport, pillar-cross 160 yards SE of church	SN 058388
Penally, sculptured stone cross in churchyard[2]	SS 117992
Pontfaen, two pillar-crosses in churchyard	SN 022340
St. David's, City Cross	SM 754253
St. Dogwell's, inscribed stone in churchyard	SM 969280
Steynton, Hang Davey Stone	SM 895146

ECCLESIASTICAL BUILDINGS

* Bosherston, St. Govan's Chapel	SR 964930
Haverfordwest Priory	SM 957152
Llandeilo, ruined church and churchyard of St. Teilo	SN 099268
Llanfyrnach, chapel and burial ground near Trehenri	SM 214303

	Grid Reference
Llawhaden Hospital	SN 068173
E Milford, St. Catherine's Chapel	SM 910057
Newtown North Church	SN 065133
St. David's, St. Justinian's Chapel	SM 723253
† St. David's, St. Non's Chapel	SM 752243
St. David's, St. Patrick's Chapel	SM 733273
† St. Dogmael's Abbey	SN 163458
Slebech Old Church	SN 032139
Steynton, Pill Priory	SM 903073

CASTLES

Angle Castle	SM 865030
Bletherston, Castell-y-frân	SN 080222
Brawdy, Pointz Castle mound	SM 830237
Camrose, Keeston Castle	SM 898196
Camrose, mound-and-bailey castle	SM 926198
Carew Castle	SN 046037
Castlebythe Castle mound	SN 021290
Castlemartin Castle	SR 915984
† Cilgerran Castle	SN 195431
Clydau, Castell Crychydd	SN 262348
Eglwyswrw, Castell Eglwyswrw	SN 139384
² Removed into the church	
Eglwyswrw, Castell Llain-fawr	SN 150374
Haverfordwest Castle	SM 953157
Hayscastle Castle mound	SM 894257
Henry's Moat, Castell Hendre	SN 045275
Lampeter Velfrey, Castell	SN 154146
Llanfair Nant-gwyn, Castell Dyffrynmawr	SN 175351
Llanfyrnach Castle mound	SN 220313
Llangolman, Castell Pengawsai	SN 110280
Llantood, Castell Pen-yr-allt	SN 158420
Llanwnda, Castell Poeth	SM 896377
† Llawhaden Castle	SN 073175
Llawhaden, Dingstopple Church mound	SN 061186
Manorbier Castle	SS 064978
Narberth Castle	SN 110144
Narberth South, Sentence Castle mound	SN 111116
Nevern, Castell Nanhyfer	SN 082401
New Moat Castle mound	SN 064253
Newton North, Castell Coch	SN 071136
Pembroke Castle	SM 982016
Pembroke Town Wall	SM 985013
Puncheston, Castell Mael	SN 010298
St. David's, Parcycastell mound-and-bailey castle	SM 745251
St. Dogwell's, Wolf's Castle mound	SM 958265
St. Ishmael's Castle mound	SM 835076
Slebech, Picton Castle mound	SN 016135
Tenby Castle	SN 137005
Tenby Town Wall	SN 134005
Wiston Castle	SN 023182

Grid
Reference

OTHER SECULAR SITES AND BUILDINGS

Angle dovecote	SM 865031
Angle, The Tower	SM 865028
Clarbeston, Knock rath	SN 039217
Eglwyswrw, Court moated site	SN 135395
Haverfordwest, mediaeval crypt at corner of Market Street and High Street	SM 952155
Hodgeston moated site	SS 029955
† Lamphey Palace	SN 018009
Minwear, Sisters' House	SN 032135
Penally, Carswell Old House	SN 098010
Penally, Whitewell	SN 033137
Rhoscrowther, Eastington Manor House	SM 901026
Rosemarket dovecote	SM 954083
† St. David's, Bishop's Palace	SM 750254
† St. David's, Close Wall	SM 749254
E St. David's, Porth y Tŵr	SM 752254
Tenby Old House	SN 135004

BRIDGES

Carew Bridge	SN 048038
Llawhaden Bridge	SN 074173
Nevern, Pontynyfer	SN 083398

MISCELLANEOUS

Angle, Chapel Bay Fort	SM 858036
Dale, Dale Point Fort	SM 824052
* Dale, West Blockhouse Fort	SM 818035
Fishguard, Castle Point old fort	SM 961378
Hakin, Fort Hubberston	SM 890054
Herbrandston, South Hook Fort	SM 870055
Herbrandston, Stack Rock Fort	SM 864049
Llanllawer, Holy Well	SM 987360
Llanrhian, Aberfelin mill	SM 835324
Llanstadwell, Fort Scoveston	SM 944066
Llanwnda, Tal-y-gaer corbelled hut	SM 893388
* Pembroke Dockyard towers	SM 963038 and 954035
Slebech, mounds on the Island	SN 033139 and 034140
Solva, lime kilns	SM 804241

NOTE: The scheduling of an ancient monument does not necessarily imply that there is public access thereto.

* Crown or Duchy property not in the charge of the Minister.

† Monuments wholly or partly in the charge of the Minister under the provisions of the Ancient Monuments Acts.

E Monuments now used for ecclesiastical purposes.

III. Some Useful Addresses

ANGLING

Pembrokeshire Anglers' Association:
Hon. Sec.: B. R. Munt, 43 High Street, Haverfordwest.
Pembrokeshire Anglers' Association (Sea Angling Section):
Hon. Sec.: B. Loosemore, 13 Addison Close, Haverfordwest.
Milford Haven Angling Club:
Hon. Sec.: D. G. James, Gwbert, Steynton Road, Milford Haven.
Newport and District Angling Association:
Hon. Sec.: Gwyn Tucker, Spring Hill, Newport, Pembs.
Pembroke and District Anglers' Club:
Hon. Sec.: T. Caveney, 1 School House, Bush Street, Pembroke.
West Wales Angling Association:
Hon. Sec.: F. Poole, Penyraber, Fishguard.

ARCHAEOLOGICAL AND HISTORICAL SOCIETIES

Cambrian Archaeological Association:
Local Sec.: W. Gwyn Thomas, St. Margaret's, Picton Road, Tenby.
Pembrokeshire Local History Society:
Hon. Sec.: Dillwyn Miles, 4 Victoria Place, Haverfordwest.

ARCHERY

Pembroke Company of Archers:
Hon. Sec.: D. R. Phillips, 128 Bush Street, Pembroke Dock.

CAMPING AND CARAVANNING

Camping Club of Great Britain and Ireland:
11 Lower Grosvenor Place, London, S.W.1.
Caravan Club of Great Britain and Ireland:
46 Brook Street, London, W.1.

CITIZENS' ADVICE BUREAU

Pembrokeshire Citizens' Advice Bureau:
4 Victoria Place, Haverfordwest.

COMMUNITY COUNCIL

Pembrokeshire Community Council:
  General Sec.: Dillwyn Miles, 4 Victoria Place, Haverfordwest.

COUNCIL FOR THE PROTECTION OF RURAL WALES

General Sec.: Simon Meade, Meifod, Montgomeryshire.
County Sec.: Patrick Stark, Haroldston Glen, Broad Haven, Haverfordwest.

FIELD CENTRES

Dale Fort:
  Warden: D. C. Emerson, Dale Fort Field Centre, Dale, Haverfordwest.
Orielton:
  Warden: Dr. Robin Crump, Orielton Field Centre, Pembroke.

GLIDING

West Wales Gliding Association:
  Hon. Sec., West Wales Gliding Association, Withybush, Haverfordwest.

MOTORING

A.A. Headquarters (Wales):
  Fanum House, Cathedral Road, Cardiff (30771).
A.A. Patrol Service Centre:
  Canaston Bridge, on A40 (Llawhaden 255).
A.A. Port Office:
  Fishguard Harbour (Fishguard 3833).
R.A.C. Headquarters (Wales):
  202 Newport Road, Cardiff (35544).
R.A.C. Port Office:
  Fishguard Harbour (Fishguard 2889).

MUSEUMS

County Museum:
  Curator: R. A. Kennedy, The Castle, Haverfordwest.
Tenby Museum:
  Hon. Curator: W. Harrison, 2 St. Catherine, Tenby.
Pembroke Castle Museum:
  Hon. Curator: A. L. J. Williams, Bridge Cottage, Lamphey, Pembroke.
Car Museum:
  Curator: C. Chester Smith, Garrison Theatre, Pembroke Dock.

NATIONAL PARK

Pembrokeshire Coast National Park Committee:
  Clerk: H. Louis Underwood, County Offices, Haverfordwest.
  Planning Officer: J. A. Price, County Offices, Haverfordwest.
National Park Information Centres:
  Haverfordwest Castle, Haverfordwest (3708).
  Town Hall, Fishguard (3484).
  City Hall, St. David's (392).
  The Norton, Tenby (2402).
  Castle Terrace, Pembroke (2148).
Pembrokeshire Countryside Unit:
  Director: J. H. Barrett, Pembrokeshire Countryside Unit, Broad
  Haven (412).

NATIONAL TRUST

Area Agent: C. H. W. Griffith, Napier House, Spilman Street,
Carmarthen.

NATURE CONSERVATION

Nature Conservancy:
  South Wales Regional Officer: P. Walters Davies, Plas Gogerddan,
  Aberystwyth.
West Wales Naturalists' Trust:
  Hon. Gen. Sec.: Dillwyn Miles, 4 Victoria Place, Haverfordwest.

RIDING AND PONY TREKKING

West Wales Riding and Trekking Centre:
  Mr. and Mrs. D. T. Moore, Newport Castle, Newport, Pembs.
Dinas Country Club Trekking Centre:
  Mrs. E. Hoyle, Dinas Country Club, Dinas Cross.
Garnwen Pony Trekking Centre:
  B. Waterson, Garnwen, Brynberian, Crymych.
Presely Pony Trekking Centre:
  Mr. and Mrs. J. Robertson-Coupar, Pantyrynn Farm, Crymych.
Trebover Riding School:
  Mrs. J. G. Lloyd-Davies, Trebover Riding School, Fishguard.
Rudbaxton Riding Centre:
  Mrs. E. H. Llewellin, Kilbarth, Rudbaxton, Haverfordwest.
Trewilym Stables:
  A. W. R. Thomas, Trewilym Farm, Hayscastle.
East Nolton Stables:
  J. Owen, East Nolton Farm, Nolton.
Starre Gorse Stables:
  B. H. Hughes, Starre Gorse, Stepaside.

East Tarr Riding Stables:
  D. H. Williams, East Tarr, St. Florence, Tenby.
Norchard Farm Riding School:
  Mrs. M. Mathias, Norchard Farm, Manorbier.

SAILING

Pembrokeshire Yachting Federation:
  Hon. Sec.: Roger Thomas, 64 The Glebe, Tenby.
Fishguard Bay Yacht Club:
  Hon. Sec.: S. B. Cox, 9 Pantycelyn, Fishguard.
Dale Yacht Club:
  Hon. Sec.: Ken Rose, Gambol Gay, Snowdrop Lane, Haverford-west.
Pembrokeshire Yacht Club:
  Hon. Sec.: Ken Ayres, 27 Wellington Road, Hakin, Milford Haven.
Neyland Yacht Club:
  Hon. Sec.: John Tee, Bandol, St. Anne's Place, Neyland.
Pembroke Haven Yacht Club:
  Hon. Sec.: M. J. Blinkthorn, Square Island, Hundleton, Pembroke.
Lawrenny Yacht Club:
  Hon. Sec.: R. Hutton, 2 Wolffe Close, Cowbridge, Glamorgan.
Pembrokeshire Racing Cruiser Club:
  Hon. Sec.: Dr. J. R. Jenkins, Red Roofs, Llangunnor, Carmarthenshire.
Tenby Sailing Club:
  Hon. Sec.: B. Shaw, 84 Upper Hill Park, Tenby.
Saundersfoot Sailing Club:
  Hon. Sec., Saundersfoot Sailing Club, The Harbour, Saunders-foot.

TOURIST OFFICES

Tourist Information Bureau: Guildhall, Tenby (2402).
Tourist Information Caravan, Kingsmoor Common, Kilgetty (Saundersfoot 3673).
Tourist Information Caravan, Penblewyn, near Narberth (Narberth 364).

WOMEN'S INSTITUTES

Pembrokeshire Federation of Women's Institutes:
  County Sec.: Mrs. M. Lidgate, 19 Pantycelyn, Fishguard.

YOUNG FARMERS' CLUBS

Pembrokeshire Federation of Y.F.C.s:
  County Sec.: M. Harries, Agriculture House, Haverfordwest.

YOUTH HOSTELS

Welsh Regional Office:
  35 Park Place, Cardiff (31370).
Hostels in Pembrokeshire Coast National Park:

Poppit Sands	SN 145488	Cardigan 2936.
Pwllderi	SM 893387	St. Nicholas 233.
Trefin	SM 840326	Croesgoch 414.
St. David's: Llaethdy	SM 739272	St. David's 345.
Newport: Maenllwyd	SN 067383	Newport 414.

GLOSSARY

aber	estuary, confluence	Abergwaun	SM 9537
afanc	beaver, monster	Beddyrafanc	SN 1034
afon	river	Afon Alun	SM 7627
allt	wood, hill, slope	Penrallt-cuch	SN 2736
ar	upon	Arberth	SN 1014
atsol	fallow	Atsol-wen	SN 1229
bach	little	Casnewydd-bach	SM 9829
bachell	corner	Fachelich	SM 7825
bâl	summit	Pen-y-bâl	SN 0441
banadl	broom (plant)	Llainbanadl	SN 1633
banc	bank, slope	Banc-du	SN 0630
barcut, barcutan	kite	Stacan Barcutan	SM 7830
bedd	grave	Bedd Morus	SN 0336
bedwen, *pl.* bedw	birch	Llanfihangel-Penbedw	SN 1837
beri	kite	Penberi	SM 7629
betws	chapel of ease	Betws	SN 0439
blaen	source, head, end	Blaenffos	SN 1937
boncath	buzzard	Boncath	SN 2038
bont	*see* pont		
breni	front, rim, prow	Y Freni Fawr	SN 2035
bro	region, country	Penfro	SM 9801
bron	breast (of hill)	Fron-las	SN 1634
brwyn	rushes	Brwynant	SM 9235
bryn	hill	Brynberian	SN 0935
bugail	shepherd	Begelly	SN 1107
bwch	buck	Penbwchdy	SM 8637
bwlch	pass	Bwlch-y-groes	SN 2436
caer, *pl.* caerau	fort, stronghold	Caerau Gaer	SN 1316
cam	crooked, bent	Y Gamlyn	SM 8024
canol	middle	Felinganol	SM 8025
capel	chapel	Capel Colman	SN 2138
carn	cairn, outcrop	Carn Llidi	SM 7328
carnedd	cairn, tumulus	Carnedd Meibion Owen	SN 0936
carreg, *pl.* cerrig	stone, rock	Carreg Edrywy	SN 0441
cas	castle	Casmael	SN 0129
castell	castle, stronghold	Castell Martin	SM 9198
cawsai	causeway	Pengawsai	SN 1716
cefn	ridge	Cefn-y-dre	SM 9635
cegin	ridge	Pengegin	SN 0334
celyn	holly	Llwyncelyn	SN 2042
celli	grove, copse	Y Gelli	SN 0819
cemais	bends, bays	Pen Cemais	SN 1250
ceunant	ravine, brook	Ceunant	SN 0437
cigfran	raven	Felin-gigfran	SN 1237
cil	corner, retreat	Cilgerran	SN 1942
cilfach	cove, creek, nook	Gilfach	SN 1613

clastir	glebe land	Clastir	SN 0941
clawdd	hedge, dyke	Clawdd-cam	SM 8728
cleddau, cleddyf	sword	Afon Cleddau	SM 9912
clegyr	rock, cairn	Clegyr Boia	SM 7325
cloch	crag, rock	Maenclochog	SN 0827
clog	cliff, rock	Y Glôg	SN 2132
clun	meadow	Clunderwen	SN 1219
clydach	torrent	Pont Clydach	SN 0739
cnwc	hillock, knoll	Pencnwc	SN 0232
coch	red	Fagwyr-goch	SN 0432
coed	trees, wood	Coedcenlas	SN 0008
coetan	quoit	Carreg Goetan	SN 0639
coety	woodland, dwelling	Goety	SN 0629
corres	female dwarf	Llwngorres	SN 0939
cors	bog, marsh	Castlemartin Corse	SR 9099
craig	rock, cliff	Craig-y-Creigwyr	SM 7227
crochan	cauldron	Pwllcrochan	SM 9202
croes	cross	Croesgoch	SM 8230
crogwydd	gallows	Cnwc-y-grogwydd	SN 0439
crug	tump, knoll	Crug-yr-hwch	SN 1632
crugiau	tumps, knolls	Crugiau Cemais	SN 1241
crwm	crooked, bent	Crymych	SN 1833
cwcwll	cowl	Quickwell	SM 7525
cwm	valley	Cwmyreglwys	SN 0140
cwmins	common	Cwmins Bach	SN 1135
cyfrwy	saddle	Carngyfrwy	SN 1432
dan	under, below	Danderi	SN 0034
dau	two	Daugleddau	SN 0009
deri	oak	Pwllderi	SM 8938
derwen	oak	Danydderwen	SN 1227
din(as)	hill-fortress	Dinas	SN 0138
dôl	meadow	Dolrannog	SN 0636
dowrog	watery	Dowrog	SM 7726
drain	thorns	Llwyn-drain	SN 1631
drum *see* trum			
drysi	brambles	Tredrysi	SN 0742
du	black	Wern-ddu	SN 1335
dwr	water	Dwr Cleifion	SM 7625
dyffryn	valley	Parc-y-dyffryn	SN 0635
efail	smithy	Efail-fach	SM 9435
eglwys	church	Eglwyswrw	SN 1438
eithin	gorse	Cefneithin	SN 0828
esgair	long ridge	Esgair-ordd	SN 1634
fach *see* bach			
faenor *see* maenor			
fagwyr *see* magwyr			
fawr *see* mawr			
feidr *see* meidr			
felin *see* melin			
foel *see* moel			
freni *see* breni			

fron *see* bron			
ffald	fold	Y Ffald	SN 0438
ffordd	road, way	Pen-ffordd	SN 0722
ffos	ditch	Ffos-y-mynach	SM 7725
ffynnon	well	Ffynnon-gain	SN 0722
gafr	goat	Blaengafren	SN 1539
ganol *see* canol			
garn *see* carn			
gawsai *see* cawsai			
gelli *see* celli			
gilfach *see* cilfach			
glan	river bank	Glandwr	SN 1928
glas	green, blue	Ffynnon-las	SN 0825
glyn	valley	Glyn-maen	SN 1435
goch *see* coch			
godir	steep, slope	Godir-y-bwch	SN 0542
gors	assembly place	Gors Fawr	SN 1329
groes *see* croes			
grug	heather	Tŷ-grug	SN 0729
gurnos	hilly place	Gurnos	SN 0634
gwaelod	bottom	Pwllgwaelod	SN 0039
gwastad	level	Gwastad	SN 0424
gwaun	moor	Cwmgwaun	SN 0135
gwennol	swallow	Plas-y-wennol	SN 1545
gwern	alder	Trewern	SN 0838
gwrach	witch	Pwll-y-wrach	SN 1045
gwrhyd	fathom, a width	Gwrhyd	SM 7627
gwylan	gull	Carreg-wylan	SN 1045
gwyn	white	Tŷ-gwyn	SM 7327
gwynt	wind	Penlan-wynt	SN 0533
haearn	iron	Pont-haearn	SN 1428
hafod	summer dwelling	Hafod Tydfil	SN 1133
haidd	barley	Haythog	SM 9921
hen	old	Henllys	SN 1039
hendre	winter dwelling	Hendre	SN 1236
hir	long	Tremaenhir	SM 8226
hydd	stag	Cnwc-yr-hydd	SN 0834
iet	gate	Tŷ'r Iet	SN 0736
isaf	lower	Treddafydd Isaf	SN 0234
las *see* glas			
lwyd *see* llwyn			
llain	narrow strip of land	Pen-llain	SN 1330
llan	church	Llan-non	SM 8331
llannerch	clearing, glade	Llannerch	SN 0535
llech	stone, rock	Llechydrybedd	SN 1043
llethr	slope	Llethr	SM 8529
llety	lodging, shelter	Llety'r Aderyn	SM 8028
llwch	lake	Lochtyrffin	SM 8529
llwyd	grey	Tŷ-llwyd	SN 0139
llwyn	tree	Llwyn-gwair	SN 0739
llygad	source	Llygadcleddau	SM 9733

			Grid Reference
llyn	lake	Blaen-llyn	SN 2432
llys	court	Llys-y-frân	SN 0424
maen	stone	Maen Sigl	SM 7327
maenor	manor	Maenorowen	SN 9336
maes	field, plain	Waun-maes	SN 0632
magwyr	wall	Fagwyr-las	SN 0332
marchog	knight	Tremarchog	SM 9035
mawr	great, big	Trellwyn-fawr	SN 0035
meidr	lane	Meidr Dywyll	SM 7526
meini	stones	Carn Meini	SN 1431
melin	mill	Felin Hescwm	SM 9938
melinau	mills	Meline	SN 1234
melindre	mill village	Velindre	SN 1039
melyn	yellow	Mynydd Melyn	SN 0135
moel	bare hill	Foel Cwmcerwyn	SN 0931
morfa	sea-marsh, fen	Morfa	SN 0541
mynach	monk	Ffos-y-mynach	SM 7725
mynachlog	monastery	Mynachlogddu	SN 1328
mynydd	mountain	Mynydd Du	SM 7626
nant	brook	Nant y Bugail	SM 9732
newydd	new	Tafarn Newydd	SN 0630
ogof	cave	Ogof Goetan	SM 7228
pall	covering, tent	Pallau	SN 1440
pant	hollow, valley	Pantyderi	SN 1637
parc	field, park	Parc y Meirw	SM 9935
pen	head, promontory	Penally	SS 1199
penglog	skull	Penybenglog	SN 1138
penrhyn	promontory	Penrhyn-ychen	SM 9838
pentre	village, homestead	Pentregalar	SN 1831
perllan	orchard	Y Berllan	SN 1339
pistyll	spout	Pistyll Meugan	SN 1737
plas	mansion, hall	Plas y Bridell	SN 1742
pont	bridge	Pont-iago	SM 9238
porth	harbour	Porthgain	SM 8132
portis	wattle fence, porch	Portis-bach	SN 1223
pren	wood	Pont-bren	SN 1139
pwll	pool, pit	Pwll-llong	SM 8836
pysgod	fish	Dinbych-y-pysgod	SN 1300
rhiw	hill	Pen-rhiw	SN 2440
rhos	moorland	Rhoscrowther	SM 9002
rhyd	ford	Glanrhyd	SN 1442
Saeson	Englishmen	Pont Saeson	SN 1135
Sais	Englishman	Iet Sais	SN 1135
strodur	pack-saddle	Pwllstrodur	SM 8663
sych	dry	Sychbant	SN 0435
tafarn	inn	Tafarn-bwlch	SN 0833
teg	fair	Pistyll-tag	SN 1631
tir	land	Tir-newydd	SN 1035
tirion	turf, country	Pant-tirion	SN 1347
traeth	beach, strand	Traeth Mawr	SM 7326
tref	town, homestead	Trefdraeth	SN 0539

			Grid Reference
tri	three	Tri-maen-trai	SM 8838
trum	ridge	Y Drum	SN 0619
trwyn	point, cape	Trwyn Bwa	SN 0542
tŷ	house	Tŷddewi	SM 7525
tyddyn	smallholding	Tyddyn Castell	SN 1338
tywarch	turf, peat	Rhosdywarch	SN 1235
tywyn	sand-dunes	Tywyn	SM 7326
uchaf	higher, upper	Pengegin uchaf	SN 0334
waun *see* gwaun			
wen *see* gwyn			
wern *see* gwern			
ŵyn	lambs	Clun-yr-ŵyn	SN 0934
y, yr, 'r	the	Yr Hendre	SN 1236
ydlan	hay guard	Ydlan Ddegwm	SN 2141
ynys	island	Ynys Cantwr	SM 7022
ysgubor	barn	Ysgubor-wen	SN 1038

BIBLIOGRAPHY

GENERAL WORKS

CAMBRENSIS, GIRALDUS. *The Itinerary through Wales* and *The Description of Wales* (1188), ed. W. Llewelyn Williams. London, 1908.

DONOVAN, E. *Tour through South Wales and Monmouthshire.* Vol. 2. London, 1805.

FENTON, RICHARD. *A Historical Tour through Pembrokeshire.* London, 1811.

FRASER, MAXWELL. *Introducing West Wales.* London, 1956.

JENNETT, SEAN. *South-West Wales.* London, 1967.

LAWS, EDWARD. *History of Little England beyond Wales.* London, 1888.

LELAND, JOHN. *The Itinerary in Wales* (1536–39), ed. L. T. Smith. London, 1906.

LOCKLEY, R. M. *Pembrokeshire.* London, 1957.

MALKIN, B. H. *The Scenery, Antiquities and Biography of South Wales.* London, 1804.

OWEN, GEORGE. *The Description of Penbrokshire* (1603), ed. Henry Owen. London, 1892.

REES, VYVYAN. *Shell Guide to South-West Wales.* London, 1963.

WIGHT, M. *Pembrokeshire and the National Park.* Tenby, 1954.

WILLIAMS, E. LLWYD. *Crwydro Sir Benfro,* I and II. Llandybie, 1960.

GEOLOGY

BASSETT, D. A., and BASSETT, M. G. (ed). *Geological Excursions in the Forest of Dean.* Cardiff, 1971.

BROWN, E. H. *Relief and Drainage of Wales: A Study in Geomorphical Development.* Cardiff, 1962.

CANTRILL, T. C., *et al. The Geology of the South Wales Coalfield,* Part XII: *The Country around Milford.* Mem. Geol. Survey G.B., 1916.

CHARLESWORTH, J. K. The South Wales End-Moraine. *Quarterly Journal of the Geological Society,* LXXXV, 335–358, 1929.

COX, A. H., *et al.* The Geology of the St. David's District. *Proceedings of the Geologists' Association,* XLI, 241–273, 1930.

DIXON, E. E. L. *The Geology of the South Wales Coalfield,* Part XIII: *The Country around Pembroke and Tenby.* Mem. Geol. Survey G.B., 1921.

EDWARDS, GEORGE. The Coal Industry in Pembrokeshire. *Field Studies,* I, 5, 33–64, 1963.

ELSDEN, J. V. The Igneous Rocks occurring between St. David's Head and Strumble Head. *Quarterly Journal of the Geological Society,* LXI, 579–585, 1905.

EVANS, W. D. The Geology of the Presely Hills, North Pembrokeshire. *Ibid.* CI, 89–95, 1945.

GEORGE, T. N. *British Regional Geology: South Wales* (Third edition). London, 1970.

GOSKAR, E. L., and TRUEMAN, A. The Coastal Plateaux of South Wales. *The Geographical Magazine,* VII, 468–477, 1934.

JEHU, T. J. The Glacial Deposits of Northern Pembrokeshire. *Transactions of the Royal Society of Edinburgh,* XLI, 53–87, 1904.

JOHN, B. S. Pembrokeshire, in Lewis, C.A. (ed.), *The Glaciations of Wales,* chapter 10, 229–265. London, 1970.

141

JOHN, B. S. Glaciation and the West Wales Landscape. *Nature in Wales*, XII, 138–155, 1971.

LEACH, A. L. The Geology and Scenery of Tenby and the South Pembrokeshire Coast. *Proceedings of the Geologists' Association*, XLIV, 1933.

MATLEY, C. A. On the Geology of part of N.E. Pembrokeshire. *Proceedings of the Birmingham Natural History and Philosophical Society*, X, 1–10, 1897.

MILLER, A. A. The 600-ft. Platform in Carmarthen and Pembrokeshire. *Geographical Journal*, XC, 148–159, 1937.

NORTH, F. J. *Sunken Cities.* Cardiff, 1957.

PRINGLE, J. The Geology of Ramsey Island. *Proceedings of the Geologists' Association*, XLI, 241–253, 1930.

STRAHAN, A., *et al. The Geology of the South Wales Coalfield*, Part XI: *The Country around Haverfordwest*. Mem. Geol. Survey G.B., 1914.

ARCHAEOLOGY AND HISTORY

ATKINSON, R. J. C. *Stonehenge.* London, 1956.

BOWEN, E. G. *The Settlements of the Celtic Saints in Wales.* Cardiff, 1954.

CHARLES, B. G. *Old Norse Relations with Wales.* Cardiff, 1934.

CLARK, G. T. *The Earls, Earldom and Castle of Pembroke.* Tenby, 1880.

DANIEL, GLYN E. *Prehistoric Chamber Tombs of England and Wales.* Cambridge, 1950.

DAVIES, DR. MARGARET. *Wales in Maps.* Cardiff, 1951.

EDWARDS, EMILY H. *Castles and Strongholds of Pembrokeshire.* Tenby, 1909.

EVANS, J. J. *Dewi Sant a'i Amseroedd.* Llandysul, 1963.

EVANS, J. T. *The Church Plate of Pembrokeshire.* London, 1905.

FOSTER, I. LL., and ALCOCK, L. *Culture and Environment.* London, 1963.

FOSTER, I. LL., and DANIEL, G. E. *Prehistoric and Early Wales.* London, 1965.

FOX, C. F. *Life and Death in the Bronze Age.* London, 1959.

FOX, C. F. *Regional Guides to Ancient Monuments.* Vol. IV: *South Wales.* London, 1954.

GREEN, FRANCIS. *West Wales Families.* Carmarthen, 1920.

GRIMES, W. F., and SAVORY, H. N. *The Prehistory of Wales.* Cardiff, 1951.

HOULDER, C., and MANNING, W. H. *Regional Archaeologies: South Wales.* London, 1966.

HOWELL, R. L. *History of the Pembroke Yeomanry.* Haverfordwest, 1959.

JAMES, G. D. *The Town and County of Haverfordwest and its Story.* Haverfordwest, 1957.

JONES, E. H. STUART. *The Last Invasion of Britain.* Cardiff, 1950.

JONES, FRANCIS. *The Holy Wells of Wales.* Cardiff, 1954.

JONES, R. W. *History of the Pembrokeshire Police Force.* Caernarvon, 1957.

LEACH, A. L. *Guide to Tenby and South Pembrokeshire.* Tenby, 1901.

LEACH, A. L. *The History of the Civic War in Pembrokeshire and its Borders.* London, 1937.

LEATHAM, DIANA. *The Story of St. David of Wales.* London, 1952.

LEWIS, E. A. *The Welsh Port Books, 1550–1603.* London, 1927.

LEWIS, E. T. *Llanfyrnach Parish Lore.* Haverfordwest, 1968.

LEWIS, E. T. *Mynachlog-ddu.* Cardigan, 1969.

LEWIS, T. P. *The Story of Wales: Pembrokeshire edition.* Llandybie, 1959.

LLOYD, KATHARINE H. *An Epitome of the Twenty-five Lords of Kemes, 1087–1914.* Carmarthen, 1930.

MILES, DILLWYN. *Newport in Pembrokeshire.* Haverfordwest, 1968.

MILES, DILLWYN. *Megalithic Monuments.* Pembrokeshire Coast National Park Information Sheet.

MILES, DILLWYN. *The Castles of Pembrokeshire.* Pembrokeshire Coast National Park Information Sheet.

MOORE, DONALD (ed). *The Land of Dyfed in Early Times.* Cambrian Archaeological Association. Cardiff, 1964.

MOORE, DONALD (ed). *The Irish Sea Province in Archaeology and History.* Cambrian Archaeological Association. Cardiff, 1970.

MORRIS, B. LL. (ed). *The Slebech Story.* Haverfordwest, 1948.

NASH-WILLIAMS, V. E. *The Early Christian Monuments of Wales.* Cardiff, 1950.

NASH-WILLIAMS, V. E. *The Roman Frontier in Wales.* Cardiff, 1954.

NASH-WILLIAMS, V. E. (ed). *A Hundred Years of Welsh Archaeology.* Cambrian Archaeological Association, 1946.

OWEN, HENRY (ed). *A Calendar of the Public Records relating to Pembrokeshire.* Vol. I: *Haverfordwest.* London, 1911.

OWEN, HENRY (ed). *A Calendar of the Public Records relating to Pembrokeshire.* Vol. III: *The Earldom of Pembroke and its Members.* London, 1918.

OWEN, HENRY. *Old Pembroke Families.* London, 1902.

PEATE, IORWERTH C. *The Welsh House.* London, 1940.

PHILLIPS, JAMES. *The History of Pembrokeshire.* London, 1909.

PHILLIPS, J. W., and WARREN, F. J. *The History of Haverfordwest with that of some Pembrokeshire Parishes.* Haverfordwest, 1914.

PHILLIPS, W. D. *Old Haverfordwest.* Haverfordwest, 1925.

PRITCHARD, EMILY M. *The History of St. Dogmael's Abbey.* London, 1907.

REES, J. F. *The Story of Milford.* Cardiff, 1954.

REES, WILLIAM. *An Historical Atlas of Wales from Early to Modern Times.* Cardiff, 1951.

STICKINGS, THOMAS G. The Story of Saundersfoot. Tenby, 1970.

THOMAS, C. (ed). *The Iron Age in the Irish Sea Provinces.* Council of British Archaeology, 9, 1970.

TIMMINS, H. THORNHILL. *Nooks and Corners of Pembrokeshire.* London, 1895.

WADE-EVANS, A. W. *Welsh Christian Origins.* Oxford, 1934.

WARBURTON, F. W. *The History of Solva.* London, 1944.

WHEELER, N. J. *The Fortification of Milford Haven and Pembroke Dock.* Pembrokeshire Coast National Park Information Sheet.

WHEELER, R. E. M. *Prehistoric and Roman Wales.* Oxford, 1925.

WILLIAMS, DAVID. *The Rebecca Riots: A Study of Agrarian Discontent.* Cardiff, 1955.

Archaeologia Cambrensis.

Transactions of the Honourable Society of Cymmrodorion.

The Pembrokeshire Historian (Journal of the Pembrokeshire Local History Society).

The National Library of Wales Journal.

The Bulletin of the Board of Celtic Studies.

Field Studies (Journal of the Field Studies Council).

Royal Commission on Ancient Monuments. *An Inventory of the Ancient Monuments in Wales and Monmouthshire.* VII: *County of Pembroke.* London, 1925.

Report of the Summer Meeting of the Royal Archaeological Institute at Tenby in 1962. *Archaeological Journal,* CXIX, 308–350, 1964.

FAUNA

BARRETT, J. H. *The Birds in Summer on the Rocky Coasts.* Pembrokeshire Coast National Park Information Leaflet.

BARRETT, J. H., and DAVIS, T. A. WARREN. *The Butterflies of Pembrokeshire.* Pembrokeshire Coast National Park Information Sheet.

BARRETT, J. H. The Birds of the Parish of Dale, including Skokholm. *Field Studies*, 1, 1–16, 1959.

BARRETT, J. H., and YONGE, C. M. *Guide to the Sea Shore* (Second edition). London, 1964.

BUXTON, E. J. M., and LOCKLEY, R. M. *Island of Skomer*. London, 1950.

CROTHERS, J. H. *Plants and Animals of Rocky Shores*. Pembrokeshire Coast National Park Information Sheet.

FISHER, JAMES. *Shell Nature Lovers' Atlas*. London, 1966.

FISHER, JAMES. *The Shell Bird Book*. London, 1966.

GOODERS, JOHN. *Where to Watch Birds*. London, 1967.

LOCKLEY, R. M., INGRAM, G. C. S., and SALMON, H. M. *The Birds of Pembrokeshire*. Cardiff, 1949.

LOCKLEY, R. M. *Shearwaters*. London, 1942.

LOCKLEY, R. M. *Letters from Skokholm*. London, 1947.

LOCKLEY, R. M. *Puffins*. London, 1953.

LOCKLEY, R. M. *The Private Life of the Rabbit*. London, 1964.

LOCKLEY, R. M. *Grey Seal, Common Seal*. London, 1966.

LOCKLEY, R. M. *The Book of Bird-Watching*. London, 1968.

LOCKLEY, R. M. *The Island*. London, 1969.

LOCKLEY, R. M. *The Naturalist in Wales*. Newton Abbot, 1970.

MATHEW, MURRAY A. *The Birds of Pembrokeshire and its Islands*. London, 1894.

Nature in Wales (Journal of the West Wales, North Wales, Brecknockshire and Radnorshire Naturalists' Trusts). 1955 *et seq.*

FLORA AND VEGETATION

CROTHERS, J. H. *Plants and Animals of Rocky Shores*. Pembrokeshire Coast National Park Information Sheet.

DALBY, D. H. The Bryophytes of the Parish of Dale. *Field Studies*, II, 283–301, 1964.

DAVIS, T. A. WARREN. *The Plants of Pembrokeshire*. Haverfordwest, 1970.

HYDE, H. A. *Welsh Timber Trees*. Cardiff, 1961.

HYDE, H. A., and WADE, A. E. *Welsh Flowering Plants*. Cardiff, 1957.

HYDE, H. A., WADE, A. E., and HARRISON, S. G. *Welsh Ferns, Clubmosses, Quillworts and Horsetails* (Fifth edition). Cardiff, 1969.

JONES, W. E., and WILLIAMS, R. The Seaweeds of Dale. *Field Studies*, II, 303–330, 1966.

MARTIN, GEORGE. The Flowering Plants and Ferns of the Dale Area. *Field Studies*, I, 21–44, 1961.

REES, F. LILLIAN. *A List of Pembrokeshire Plants*. Haverfordwest, 1955.

LAND USE AND FARMING

ASHBY, ERIC, and EVANS, I. L. *The Agriculture of Wales*. Cardiff, 1944.

BOWEN, E. G. A Study of Rural Settlements in South-West Wales. *Geographical Teacher*, 1926.

CARTER, H. Urban Grades and Spheres of Influence in South-West Wales. *Scottish Geographical Magazine*, LXXI, 43–62, 1955.

CARTER, H. *The Towns of Wales: A Study in Urban Geography*. Cardiff, 1965.

DAVIES, MARGARET. *Report of the Land Utilisation Survey of Britain*, Part 32: *Pembrokeshire*. London, 1939.

DRESSER, B. J. Land Use and Farm Practice in the Parish of Dale. *Field Studies*, I, 17–39, 1959.

GILPIN, MARGARET C. Population Changes round the shores of Milford Haven from 1800 to the present day. *Field Studies*, I, 23–36, 1960.

HASSALL, CHARLES. *General View of the Agriculture of the County of Pembroke.* London, 1794.

JONES, A. M. *Rural Industries of England and Wales.* IV: *Wales.* Oxford, 1927.

PLACE-NAMES

CHARLES, B. G. *Non-Celtic Place-Names in Wales.* London, 1938.

DAVIES, ELWYN (ed). *Rhestr o Enwau Lleoedd: A Gazetteer of Welsh Place-Names.* Cardiff, 1958.

HARRIES, P. V. *South Pembrokeshire Dialect and Place-Names.* Tenby, 1960.

MILES, DILLWYN. *The Meaning of some Pembrokeshire Place-Names.* Pembrokeshire Coast National Park Information Sheet.

MORRIS, W. MEREDITH. *A Glossary of the Demetian Dialect of North Pembrokeshire.* Tonypandy, 1910.

Index

146

The Country Code

GUARD AGAINST ALL RISK OF FIRE

Plantations, woodlands and heaths are highly inflammable: every year acres burn because of casually dropped matches, cigarette ends or pipe ash.

FASTEN ALL GATES

Even if you found them open. Animals can't be told to stay where they're put. A gate left open invites them to wander, a danger to themselves, to crops and to traffic.

KEEP DOGS UNDER PROPER CONTROL

Farmers have good reason to regard visiting dogs as pests; in the country a civilised town dog can become a savage. Keep your dog on a lead wherever there is livestock about, also on country roads.

KEEP TO THE PATHS ACROSS FARM LAND

Crops can be ruined by people's feet. Remember that grass is a valuable crop too, sometimes the only one on the farm. Flattened corn or hay is very difficult to harvest.

AVOID DAMAGING FENCES, HEDGES AND WALLS

They are expensive items in the farm's economy; repairs are costly and use scarce labour. Keep to recognised routes, using gates and stiles.

LEAVE NO LITTER

All litter is unsightly, and some is dangerous as well. Take litter home for disposal; in the country it costs a lot to collect it.

SAFEGUARD WATER SUPPLIES

Your chosen walk may well cross a catchment area for the water supply of millions. Avoid polluting it in any way. Never interfere with cattle troughs.

PROTECT WILD LIFE, WILD PLANTS AND TREES

Wild life is best observed, not collected. To pick or uproot flowers, carve trees and rocks, or disturb wild animals and birds, destroys other people's pleasure as well.

GO CAREFULLY ON COUNTRY ROADS

Country roads have special dangers: blind corners, high banks and hedges, slow-moving tractors and farm machinery or animals. Motorists should reduce their speed and take extra care; walkers should keep to the right, facing oncoming traffic.

RESPECT THE LIFE OF THE COUNTRYSIDE

Set a good example and try to fit in with the life and work of the countryside. This way good relations are preserved, and those who follow are not regarded as enemies.

Printed in England for Her Majesty's Stationery Office by Headley Brothers Ltd, 109 Kingsway
London WC2B 6PX and Ashford, Kent
Dd.503626 K80 2/73

Other illustrated
guides in the
National Park Series

Peak District	**45p**	$(51\frac{1}{2}p)$
Northumberland	$37\frac{1}{2}\textbf{p}$	(45p)
Exmoor	$42\frac{1}{2}\textbf{p}$	(50p)
Brecon Beacons	**50p**	$(56\frac{1}{2}p)$
Yorkshire Dales	**45p**	$(51\frac{1}{2}p)$

Prices in brackets include postage

Please send your orders or requests for free lists of titles or guide-
books to Her Majesty's Stationery Office, P6A (ZD) Atlantic House,
Holborn Viaduct, London EC1P 1BN

 **HMSO BOOKS**